Balloon Masterpieces:

A Collection of Over 100 Captivating Sculptures

Copyright
Copyright © 2023
All rights reserved.

CONTENTS

One **Magic Balloons**
Two **Pumping Up**
Three **Getting to Know Your Balloons**
Four **Let's Do the Twist!**
    The Pinch and Twist
    Lock Twist
    Fold Twist
Five **From Puppies to Giraffes**
    Basic Dog
    Dachshund
    Cat
    Basic Horse
    Giraffe
    Rabbit
    Mouse
Six **Using the Fold Twist**
    Three-Twist Dog
    Giraffe, Dachshund, and Cat Using Fold Twists
    Elephant
    Alligator
    Flower
    Sword
    Birds and Bees
Seven **Bears, Poodles, and Floppy-Eared Dogs**
    The Ear Twist
    Teddy Bear
    Poodle
    Floppy-Eared Dog

        Floppy-Eared Dachshund
        Sitting Cat
        Sitting Rabbit

Eight   The Roll-Through
        Swan
        Stegosaurus
        Detailed Horse
        Rubber Ducky
        Turtle or Ladybug

Nine   Unusual Twists
        The Tulip Twist
        Tulip
        Pig
        Inserts or Seeds
        Hot Dog with a Meatball Inside (aka Pregnant Pup)
        Split Twists and Pop Twists
        Letters and Numbers
        Monkey
        Airplane
        Motorcycle
        Spiral
        Cobra

Ten   Hats
        Headband
        Flapper Hat
        Feather Headdress
        Daniel Boone Hat
        Pilot's Headset
        Space Helmet
        Space Helmet with Pom-Pom
        Wild Antennae
        Hairy Hats

        Bike Helmet
        Crown
        King's Crown and Queen's Crown
        Super-Duper Hat
        Twist Hat
        Braided Hat (Aladdin's Turban)
        Princess Hat
        Lightning Bolt Hat
        Flower Hat
        Spiral Hat
        Super Space Hat
        Mouse Ears
        Octopus Hat
        Monkey in a Tree Hat
        Spartan Hat
        Heart Hat

Eleven Heart Designs
        The Basic Heart Shape
        Lovebirds on a Heart
        Heart Wand
        Butterfly
        Heart Flower
        Rosebud

Twelve Multiple-Balloon Designs
        The Safety Bubble
        Penguin
        Lobster
        Mermaid
        Bicycle
        Octopus
        Spider
        Little Red Wagon

Thirteen Balloon Cartoons
    Big Ol' Bear
    Big Ol' Cat
    Crazy Rabbit
    Coyote or Wolf
    Mouse
    Dippy Duck
    Beaks, Wings, and Tails
    Finished Stork, Eagle, Rooster, Pelican, Magpie, Woodpecker
    Rudolph the Red-Nosed Reindeer
    Martian

Fourteen The Business of Balloons
    Working for Tips
    Balloon Vending
    Balloon Decorating
    Using Balloons as an Entertainer
    Basics

    The Last Word
    Balloon Suppliers

Chapter One

Magic Balloons

One of the first questions a bystander might ask a balloon artist is "Are they special balloons?" The answer is "Yes and no." Most balloons used for sculpting are made out of a type of rubber called latex. The quality of the latex may vary between manufacturers, but basically all latex balloons have the same stretching and twisting properties.

Though sculpting balloons are made of similar material, they are not all shaped the same. Different balloons are designed to expand to specific shapes and sizes when they are inflated. Some will be big and round; others will be small and round. Some will be long and skinny or short and fat. There is a variety of unusual, specific-shaped balloons that include hearts, bear heads, bee bodies, flowers, donuts, spirals, and caterpillars. There are even balloons that are designed to link end to end for various purposes and many that are produced with printed images or patterns. With so many styles of balloons available, it is important to know that it is the shape and size of the balloon, more than any other factor, that will dictate what you can do with it once you begin twisting.

The long, skinny balloons known as animal, twisty, or pencil balloons are those designed specifically for sculpting; they come in various sizes depending on your creative needs. They are officially named with numbers that describe their width and length after they are inflated. The most commonly used balloon is the 260. The "2" refers to the width, which is approximately two inches in diameter, and the "60" refers to the length, which is approximately sixty inches, end to end. Most of the designs in this book require 260s, unless otherwise stated. In many cases, the 260 can be substituted with balloons of varying widths and lengths to create the same designs in smaller or larger scale.

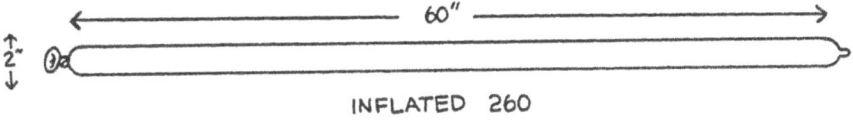
INFLATED 260

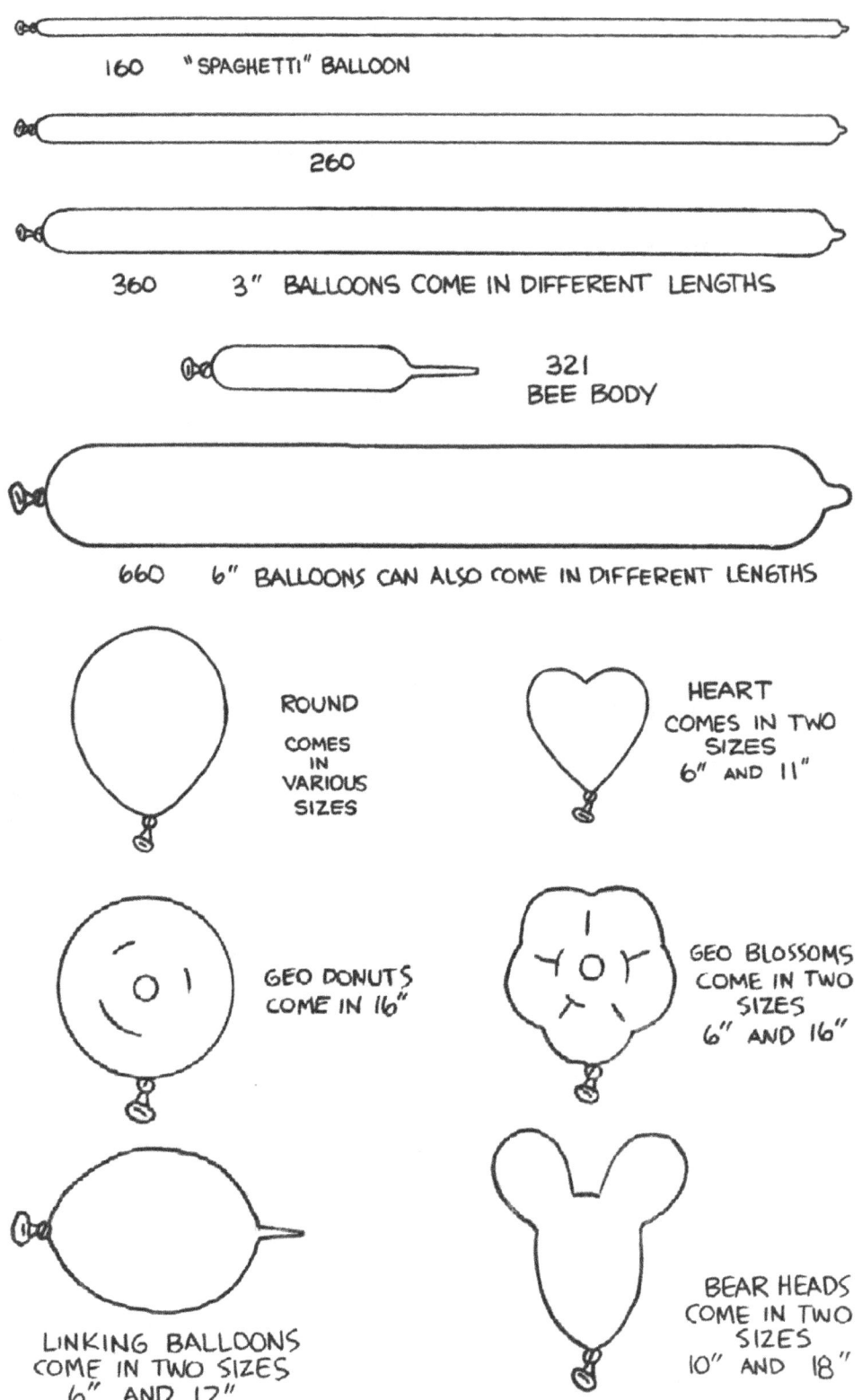

As you discover more about designing with balloons, you will realize that you can incorporate almost any balloon shape into some type of design. Because of this, I am including this handy-dandy guide to most of the popular balloon styles. They are all shown inflated.

Balloons are made by several different manufacturers, and some may not make all styles of balloons. Experiment with a variety of brands to find the balloons you enjoy working with the most. Fortunately, because balloons have become so popular, it is now easier than ever to find the many different styles and brands of balloons. Good places to look for balloons are party stores, toy stores, magic shops, and the internet. It is best to buy balloons by the bag. Most manufacturers bag balloons in quantities of 50 and 100 and sell them in assorted or solid colors.

As you begin to use larger quantities of balloons, you will certainly want to order from balloon distributor websites that offer bulk prices and shipping discounts. How you store your balloons will also become important to you. Latex balloons are naturally biodegradable and, given time, will eventually lose their durable qualities. They may acquire small holes or become brittle, making them more likely to pop. Light and heat do the most harm and will be sure to deteriorate balloons quicker than usual. To prevent balloons from going "stale," store them loosely in a cool, dark place. Many balloon artists prefer to store their balloons in a refrigerator to keep them "fresh."

When you are working with your balloons, be conscious of your environment! The weather will have instant effects on your balloons if it is too hot or too cold. Try to work in the shade, and store your balloons in an insulated pouch or container. Also be aware of the effects that you are having on the environment. Always clean up after yourself, leaving your work area as it was when you arrived. Broken or discarded balloons can leave a very unsightly mess that can be dangerous to small children and animals that may try to eat balloon scraps.

Note that there are other types of balloons made of mylar that are very popular for their shimmery foil surface and wide variety of shapes and printed color images. These balloons are not meant for twisting, so I will not cover them extensively in this book, but, along with latex balloons, they can be incorporated into some very creative designs frequently used by balloon decorators.

Chapter Two

Pumping Up

Blowing up the balloon is the most important part of making a balloon design. The amount of air that is used will determine the initial size and shape of the balloon and how much twisting can be done to it. This is true of every style of balloon but is most important when using the long, skinny, twisty balloons which we will refer to as 260s throughout the rest of this book.

Most of us have inflated round balloons by mouth and have found it to be not very difficult to do. Blowing up a 260 by mouth, however, because of its narrow shape, is much more difficult, so much so that it is not recommended. Blowing up 260s by mouth may appear flashy, and many professionals prefer to inflate them this way, but it subjects the balloon artist to so many health risks that it is not worth doing. So if you can't do it, don't feel discouraged!

Today there are many pumps that are available specifically for inflating 260s. The easiest pumps to find in stores are hand pumps. They can be found at most party or balloon stores and can inflate a 260 fully with about three or four strokes. These pumps come in fun colors and are made by a number of different manufacturers. They are generally inexpensive. Some are more durable than others, so be selective when you buy. A good rule of thumb is that shiny plastic is less durable and more likely to break. The better hand pumps will allow you to open them up. Your pump will last longer with proper maintenance, so keep it clean and lubricate and inspect gaskets and O-rings regularly. It is also a good idea to have a backup pump available should your pump stop working in the middle of a project or performance.

Because of their relatively small size, hand pumps can be carried easily in a large pocket or a balloon bag. This has made them popular with clowns and other strolling entertainers. Some like to attach a strap to their hand pump and hang it over their shoulder while they twist.

Another hand pump that is very easy to find is the sport-ball pump. It can be found in almost any store that sells sporting goods. This pump is small and narrow and usually comes in packages with two types of nozzles: a needle for inflating basketballs and footballs (also great for inflating the tiny 160 balloons) and a cone-shaped plastic nozzle for inflating vinyl toys and balloons. Always check for this balloon nozzle before purchasing this pump, because some manufacturers do not include it in the package. This pump is also usually inexpensive. It is usually made of plastic but has a metal shaft that makes it more durable. This is the smallest of the hand pumps and requires more strokes to inflate a 260.

The pumps that have been mentioned are the most popular and the easiest to find in stores. They are perfect for beginners and professionals alike, but they may not be the best pumps for every occasion. As you grow as a balloon artist, you may find that you are inflating large volumes of balloons and getting too much exercise! Many professionals will find themselves with long lines of children waiting for balloons, in which case the hand pump is not fast enough to do the job. Fortunately, other pumps exist to meet these demands.

The upright pump was originally designed by Tom Myers for use by clowns and magicians. Now, this type of pump is made by a few different sources and is available online and through magic and balloon distributors. These durable pumps, made of PVC or another strong plastic, stand on the ground and are about waist high. The user pulls up then pushes down for air, which comes out of a nozzle at the top of the pump, inflating a 260 easily with just one stroke. These pumps really get the job done and are useful for establishing your work area when working in a crowd.

Other pumps that are great for volume twisting are electric pumps. Many are made for different purposes than balloon sculpting, and some are not strong enough to inflate 260s, even though they may inflate other types of balloons easily. Many of these pumps need to be plugged into an outlet, while others are battery-operated and rechargeable. The battery-operated pumps are usually very portable, and some can be worn in a hip pouch. The duration of power may be different from brand to brand, but it is always advisable to have a backup battery. Electric pumps almost always make some type of noise, some louder than others. You may wish to search for a type that is compatible with your working conditions.

A final source for inflating your balloons is compressed air or gas from a tank. Most of us are familiar with helium tanks for inflating balloons intended to float. Some people like to use compressed air for its silence and speed, though it usually requires a large tank, a hose, and some type of nozzle with a trigger. Small tanks or cartridges can be used in special circumstances and can sometimes be concealed to make a balloon seem to magically inflate.

One note about helium: Resist the temptation to inflate your 260 with helium and expect your creations to float. 260s do not contain enough cubic inches of space in relation to the weight of the latex to allow your balloon to do much more than hover slightly. Believe me, I tried.

Remember, each pump is best suited for certain circumstances. Learn to use them to your advantage.

Chapter Three

Getting to Know Your Balloons

Before you begin any balloon creation, it is important to know the balloon or balloons that you are working with. The balloon becomes your partner in the creation, and you must know that you can depend on it and work with it. Style, color, quality, and freshness all become important factors that must be inspected before starting your design.

Style or type of balloon, of course, depends on what you plan to create. As I mentioned earlier, most of the designs in this book are made with 260s, so we will be focusing on that style of balloon in this section.

Color is usually easy to determine. You may choose a color just because you like it, or because it will help to define your design, by making a pig pink or a swan white, for example. Most colors will be easy to notice in a bag of balloons. Some of the darker colors, like purple, green, and black, however, may be harder to identify because, uninflated, their pigment is condensed and they will all appear to be black. They can be more easily distinguished by inflating a small bubble or by stretching the balloon near the open end to reveal the color. As you develop as a balloon artist, you may wish to buy balloons in packs of solid colors, especially for colors you use most. You will notice that manufacturers make different shades of each color and that some are easier to identify uninflated. You may choose to work with a different shade of green, purple, blue, or brown just to avoid confusion with other balloons that may appear to be black when uninflated.

The quality of the balloon you are using may not always be easy to determine until it has been inflated. Before inflating, however, look for defects, which may appear as tears, holes, or clumps of latex. A balloon with these imperfections is going to break, so discard it immediately. Even after close examination, however, it is not always possible to detect imperfections before inflating. Always be cautious when inflating, being careful to keep the balloon away from eyes, which can be harmed by bits of rubber thrown from an exploding balloon. Once the balloon has been inflated, check for leakage of air. If your balloon has leakage, you will see the balloon slowly shrinking or hear a little hissing noise. You should release the remaining air and discard the balloon.

You may discover that all the balloons of a certain color in a bag are much weaker than balloons of the other colors. Red balloons from one bag, for example, may almost always pop while you are twisting them, but the other colors all seem fine. If you see this trend, avoid using the color in question. It may indicate a bad batch. Most likely, the next bag you open will not have that problem.

Balloons that are not fresh will give you the most trouble. It is hard to tell just by looking at them if balloons are old. They may have some discoloration, and they may feel limp or less resilient than new balloons, but you *will* know for sure when you inflate them! You will have a high percentage of breakage, and no single color will be a factor. It is time to buy new balloons!

Be comfortable with the balloons that you are using. Relax and get over the fear that they may break. I can guarantee that you will break balloons. Expect it. You will break less if you are not tense from worrying about them breaking!

Once you have selected a healthy 260, hold it out and wiggle it. You have just created your first balloon animal: a Worm! This may seem silly, but that is how simple it is to imagine and suggest animals and objects with balloons. Notice that your balloon, like the worm, has two ends: the mouth, which you will blow the air into, and the tail, which is the section that will inflate.

Do not stretch your balloon! Stretching weakens the latex. It is a practice that makes it easier for someone to inflate by mouth, but it sacrifices the quality of the balloon for the sake of theatrics. If you were to take a balloon and stretch just about an inch of it in the center, that weaker part would inflate first when you pumped air into the balloon. It is for this reason that when checking for color, you should only stretch the area near the mouth of the balloon.

Now that you have selected, inspected, and are comfortable with your 260, place the mouth of your balloon over the nozzle of your pump. Continue to hold the balloon on the nozzle so that the air does not blow it off when you begin to pump. As you start to pump, try to channel the air so that the balloon begins to inflate about an inch away from the mouth of the balloon. This will give you plenty of room to tie the knot.

Inflate the balloon until it is about eighteen inches long with about a six-inch tail. Continue to hold the balloon tightly at the open end so that no air is released, and remove it from the pump. The inflated area of the 260 is the "body" of the balloon. The uninflated portion is still considered the tail.

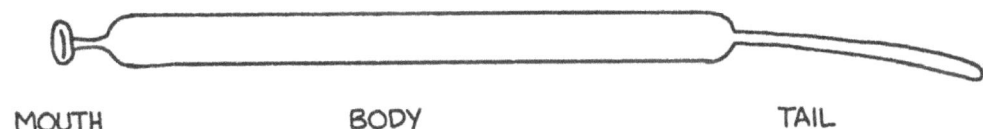

MOUTH   BODY   TAIL

After you have removed the balloon from the pump, release a small amount of air from the balloon. This is called burping, and you will know why when you hear the sound that the balloon makes! The balloon is burped to release some of the pressure in it so that it will not break as easily. Do not release too much air, or there will not be enough tension in the latex to make an effective sculpture. With practice you will develop a feel for how much air is appropriate. Some balloon artists prefer to work "tight" and release no air. They are careful to work the air back into the tail of the balloon as they twist. This relaxes the balloon as they work.

After you have inflated and burped your balloon, it is time to tie a knot in it so that the air can no longer escape. Tying a knot is simple. Continue to hold the balloon so that the air can't escape. With the other hand, stretch the mouth away from the body of the balloon and create a loop around one or two of the fingers with which you are pulling. Cross the stretched area over itself and tuck the mouth of the balloon back through the opening in the loop. Pull gently on the mouth of the balloon, tightening the knot. Do not pull the knot too tight, because you may damage the balloon.

This is just one way of tying the knot. If you have a way that works better for you, use it! As with anything creative, there is not just one right way to do it.

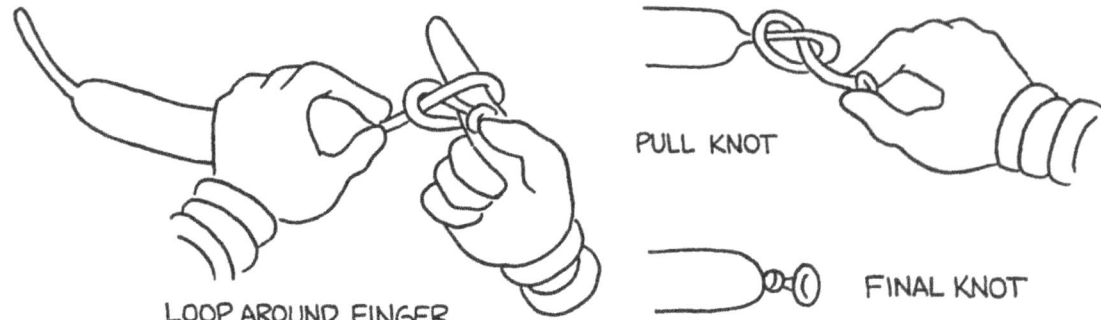

Chapter Four

Let's Do the Twist!

Transforming your partially inflated balloon into a recognizable design requires creating bubbles of the same or different sizes, then locking them together and arranging them in a particular order. The bubbles become your building blocks with which to create. There are only a limited number of ways to twist, bend, or lock bubbles, yet so much can be created with them—and you are in control!

Before we begin with any designs, we should warm up with some twisting exercises. Pick up your partially inflated balloon and start at the knotted end. Focus on a spot about three inches from the knot and gently squeeze it between the thumb and forefinger of one hand. With your other hand, grasp the remaining portion of the balloon near where you are squeezing and twist the body of the balloon away from you, turning it three to five times to ensure the quality of the bubble you are creating. Continue to hold both ends of the balloon, or your bubble will unwind. This method of creating a bubble is called the *pinch and twist*.

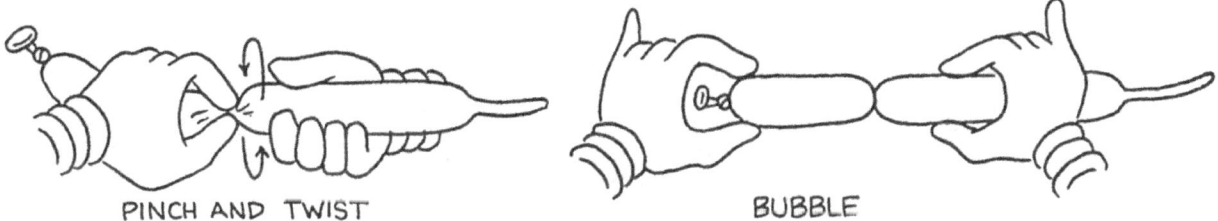

PINCH AND TWIST   BUBBLE

Holding your first bubble using the fourth and fifth finger of the hand that it is in, repeat the pinch and twist to create a second bubble. Do not let go of the first bubble or the remaining body of the balloon! Make a few bubbles in this fashion. Try to make all of the bubbles the same size. You will notice that with each bubble you make, the tail of the balloon gets shorter as the air is displaced into it. As you continue twisting, the tail will eventually disappear altogether, making it impossible to create more bubbles.

The consecutive bubbles that you have created are called a *chain*. The chain will come undone if you let go of the end bubbles. The points where the bubbles connect to each other are called *joints* and are used to lock bubbles together. Find the first joint in your chain and align it with the last joint and twist about three times. You can now let go; your bubbles are locked in place. This is a *lock twist*.

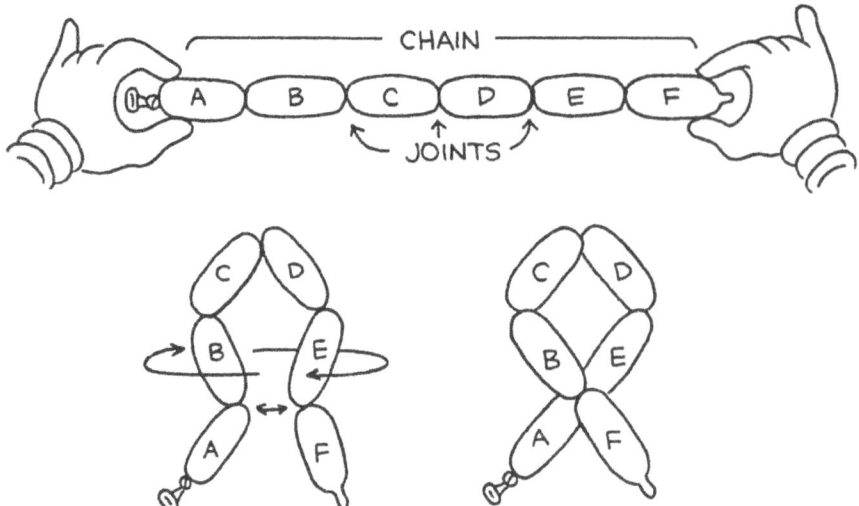

Practice making chains with different numbers of bubbles and locking them together. Make groups of locked chains on one balloon and you will begin to see how shapes come together.

Bubbles can be folded and locked together, creating loops of different sizes. To practice, start with a small bubble about one to two inches in length, then make a second bubble that is about seven to ten inches. Fold the second bubble in half, locking the joints where the bubble begins and ends. This is a *fold twist*. A larger version of the fold twist is a *loop*; this is used to make hats and some other larger designs. Practice making loops of different sizes.

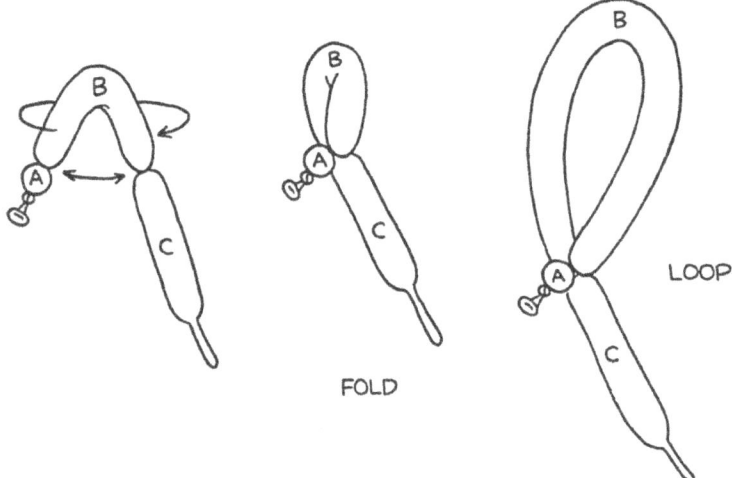

These exercises will help you to familiarize yourself with balloons and to relax and feel more confident as you learn the designs in this book. What you have practiced so far are the most fundamental skills of a balloon artist. The balloon artist uses these basics over and over, modifying them to create hundreds of designs.

Later in this book we will examine other techniques that expand on the basics to help create some unusual designs.

Chapter Five

From Puppies to Giraffes

The most commonly made balloon design is the basic animal. It is made entirely of lock twists. This design, like most four-legged animals, has a head with ears, a neck, a body, four legs, and a tail. It is the ultimate generic animal. Some beginning yet clever balloon artists often pass this design off as a dog, cat, bear, horse, hippo, or any other animal that might come close! This can actually be very amusing, since most children, with their great imaginations, can often see almost any animal that a balloon artist might suggest their creation is.

The basic animal balloon is generally accepted to be a puppy or a dog. It can, however, with some minor changes, be converted into a very convincing cat, mouse, giraffe, horse, dachshund, or rabbit! The key to these transformations is bubble proportion. The size relationships that the bubbles have to each other become the determining factor for animal recognition.

The following designs are all made with three sets of lock twists that each involve three bubbles. The only difference between them is the size of their bubbles. Learn to make the Basic Dog and you can make all of them.

BASIC DOG

The Basic Dog or Puppy can be made of bubbles that are all approximately the same size. Select a 260 and inflate it, leaving about five or six inches of tail. The body of the balloon will be about twenty-four inches in length. Burp the balloon and tie the knot. Make three bubbles that are each about two to three inches long. A good measuring tool is the width of three fingers.

Lock twist the bubbles as shown. You have created the head and ears of your Dog.

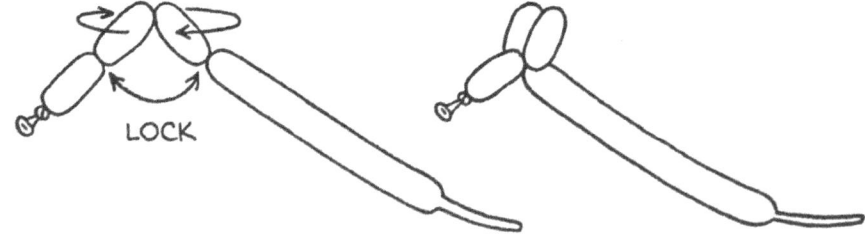

Repeat this step with three more bubbles of the same size and you will create the neck and front legs of the Dog.

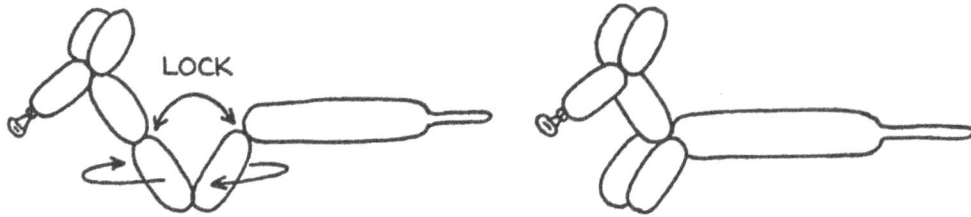

To complete the Dog, repeat with three more bubbles of the same size, creating the body and back legs of the Dog. The remaining portion of the balloon, including the tail of the balloon, becomes the tail of the Dog.

The following is a simplified diagram of how the dog is constructed. It is broken down into three parts: (1) the Bubble Chart, which shows all of the bubbles that are used, identifies each bubble with a letter, approximates the size of each bubble, and notes which joints the bubbles will lock at; (2) the Locking Diagram, which illustrates how the locks should come together. This continues to use the identifying letters for each bubble and uses arrows to indicate where joints should meet; and (3) the Complete Design, which is broken down into two images: one with identifying letters showing where each bubble should be and one with no letters and suggested markings if you should choose to decorate your creation with a permanent marker.

BUBBLE CHART

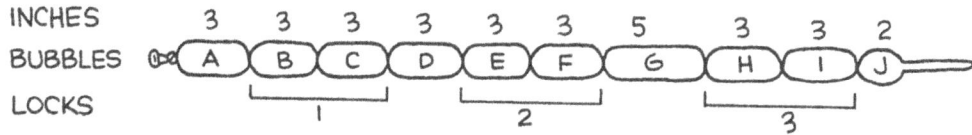

LOCKING DIAGRAM

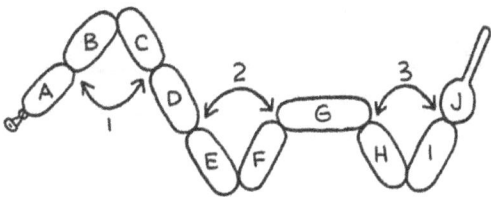

COMPLETE DESIGN

Most of the designs in this book will be accompanied by this type of diagram. New twists will be explained and then incorporated into this type of diagram. Always take careful note of the bubble sizes and their proportion to other bubbles in the design.

The following design diagrams show how you can transform the Basic Dog design into other animals by changing bubble proportion.

DACHSHUND

Inflate a 260, leaving about three inches of tail.

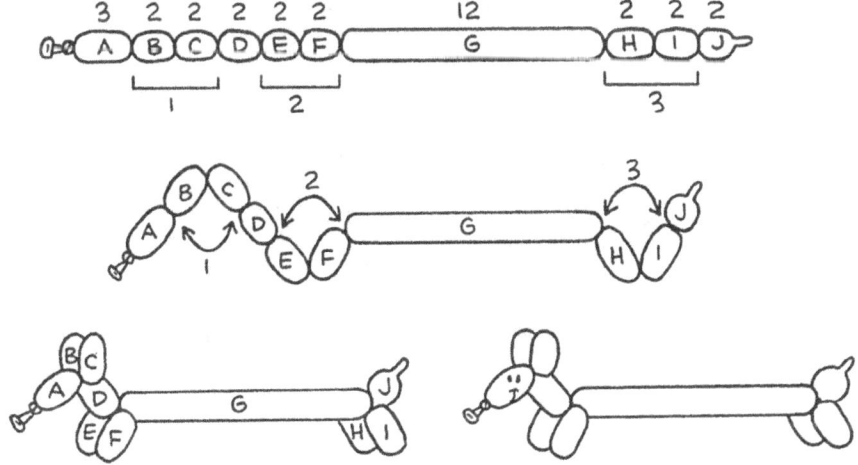

Shorter legs and longer body distinguish the Dachshund from the Basic Dog.

CAT

Inflate a 260, leaving about three inches of tail.

Shorter ears and longer tail distinguish the Cat from the Basic Dog.

BASIC HORSE

Inflate a 260, leaving about three inches of tail.

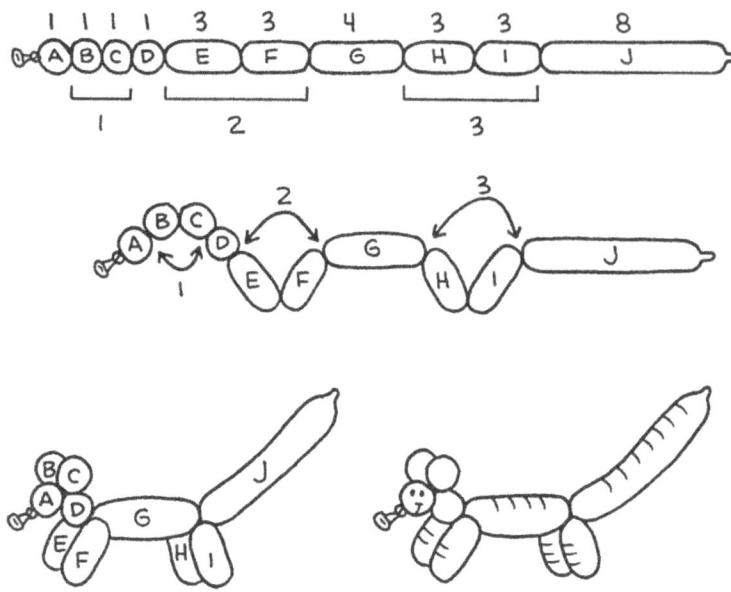

Smaller ears and longer legs distinguish the Basic Horse from the Basic Dog.

A more detailed horse design will be diagrammed later in this book.

GIRAFFE

Inflate a 260, leaving about three inches of tail.

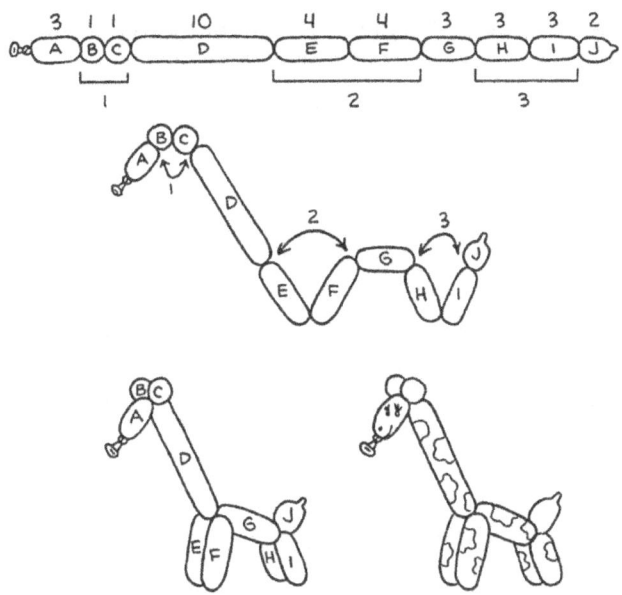

Smaller ears and much longer neck distinguish the Giraffe from the Dog.

RABBIT

Inflate a 260, leaving about three inches of tail.

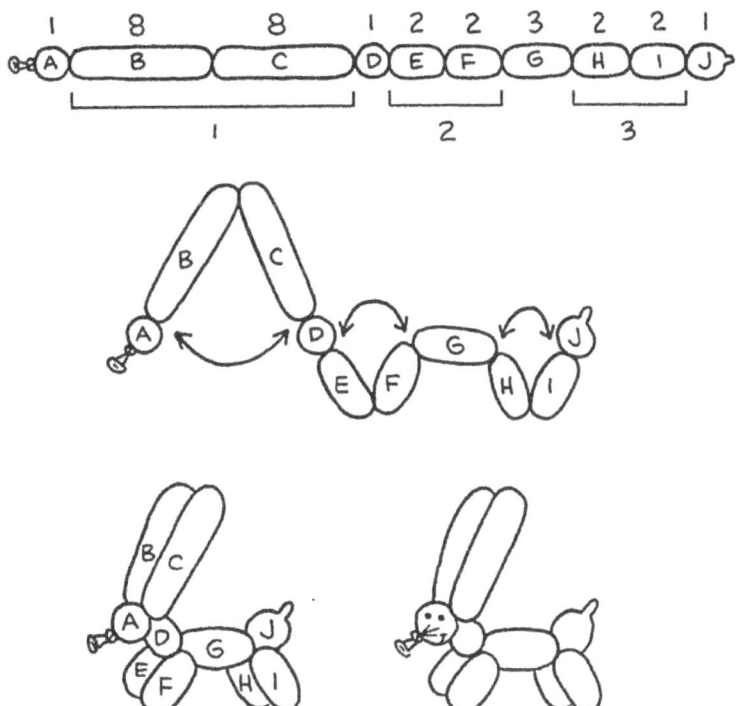

Longer ears and shorter legs and tail distinguish the Rabbit.

MOUSE

Inflate a 260 so that the body of the balloon is only about five to six inches long. The tail of the balloon will be about nine inches long.

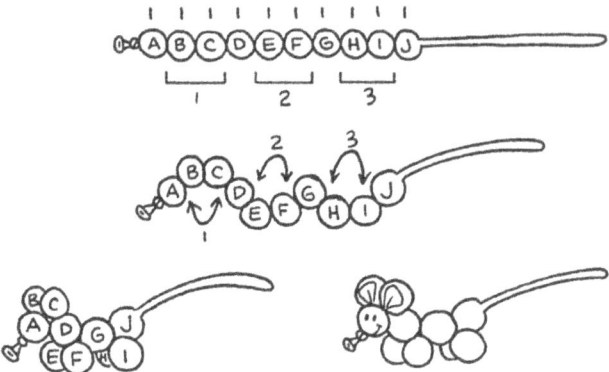

The small size of the figure and the use of the balloon's long tail distinguish the Mouse.

Now that you have made the Mouse design, you can more easily see that the tail of the balloon can play an important part in the design. In the Basic Dog it is desirable to have about two inches of balloon tail left to resemble the wagging tail of a puppy. In the other designs, however, the tail of the balloon should be minimal to nonexistent. You may have noticed that to accomplish this, more air was added to the balloon, making the tail of the balloon shorter before we even began twisting.

Too many variables make it difficult to exactly determine perfect measurements concerning bubble sizes, tail length, and body length. Experiment to find which measurements give you the best results, then develop a measuring tool like finger widths or hand widths so that you can quickly and accurately size your measurements with consistency.

Proportion is your most important tool. Practice making legs and ears even in size, striving for symmetry in your designs. Soon your balloons will be beautiful and uniform, and you will be proud to present them as your work!

Chapter Six

Using the Fold Twist

The fold twist is used to make some of the quickest balloon designs and can even be used to simplify the Basic Dog. In Chapter 4 we reviewed how to make a fold twist by bending a long bubble in half and locking it at its end joints. I had intentionally shown the more detailed way of constructing a fold twist so that you would understand its mechanics, but now I would like to show you a more efficient way while explaining how to make a dog with just three twists.

THREE-TWIST DOG

Inflate your 260, leaving about three to four inches of tail, and tie a knot in the balloon. Beginning with the knotted end, measure about six inches, or two hand widths. At this point, fold the balloon, creating a long side and a short side. Hold both sides together. Find a point in the middle of the short side. Grasp both sides at this point. Gently squeeze and twist the folded portion away from you a few times as you would when making a pinch twist. The fold twist is now locked together, and you have made the head and ears of a Three-Twist Dog!

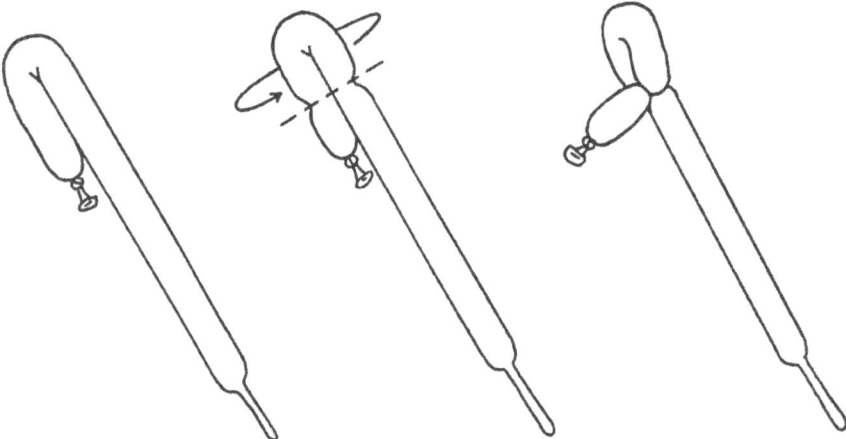

You will repeat this step two more times, as you did with the lock twists that made the Basic Dog, creating next the neck and front legs, then the body and the back legs, leaving the remaining portion of the balloon as the dog's tail. The following is a diagram of the Three-Twist Dog.

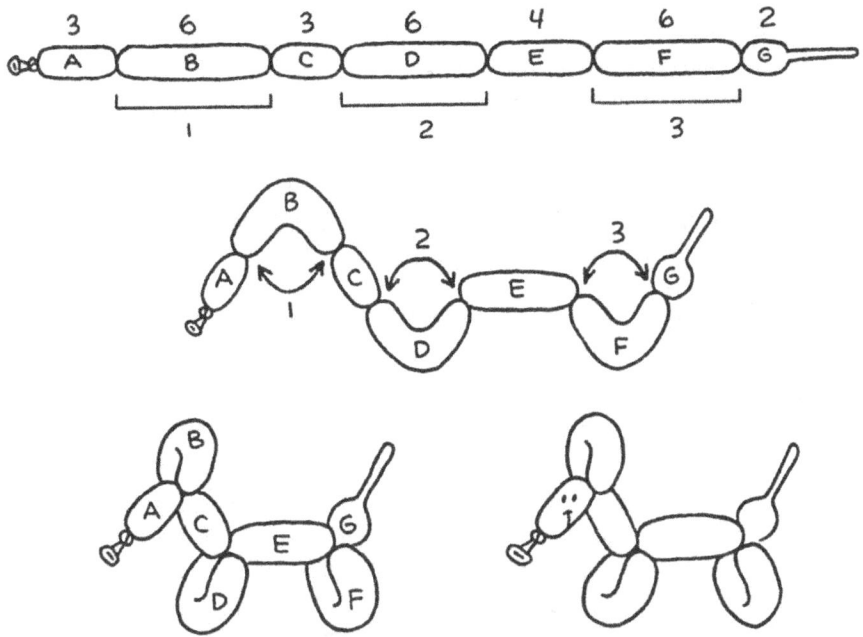

You can see that the Three-Twist Dog looks very similar to the Basic Dog but is much quicker to make. Practice changing proportions to make some of the other basic animals.

Giraffe

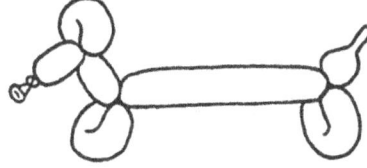

Dachshund

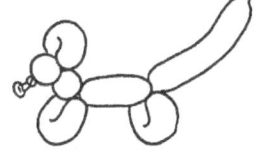

Cat

ELEPHANT

The Elephant combines both the fold and the lock twists. Two consecutive fold twists are used to create his big ears. Use the following diagram and carefully note measurements, especially for his long trunk.

Inflate a 260, leaving about three inches of tail. Tie a knot and begin!

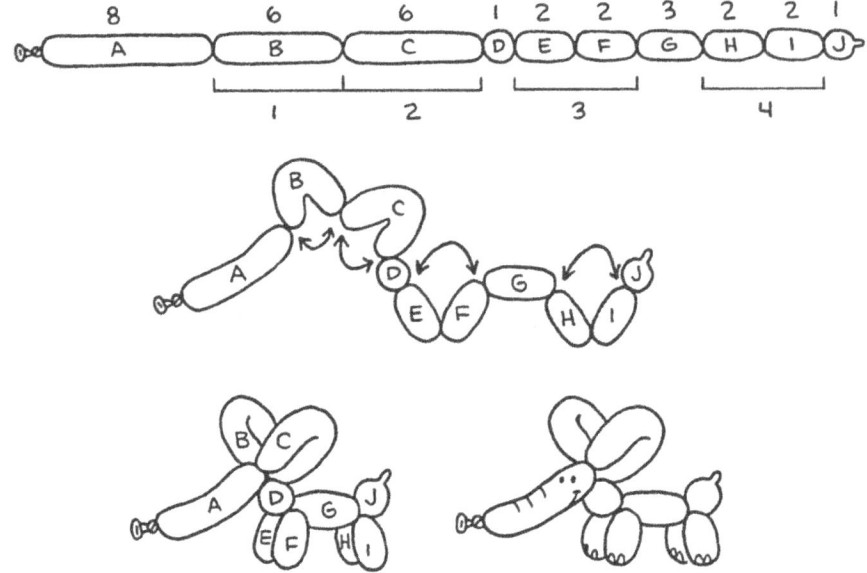

ALLIGATOR

The Alligator design uses fold twists for each leg.

Inflate a 260, leaving about two to three inches of tail. Tie the knot.

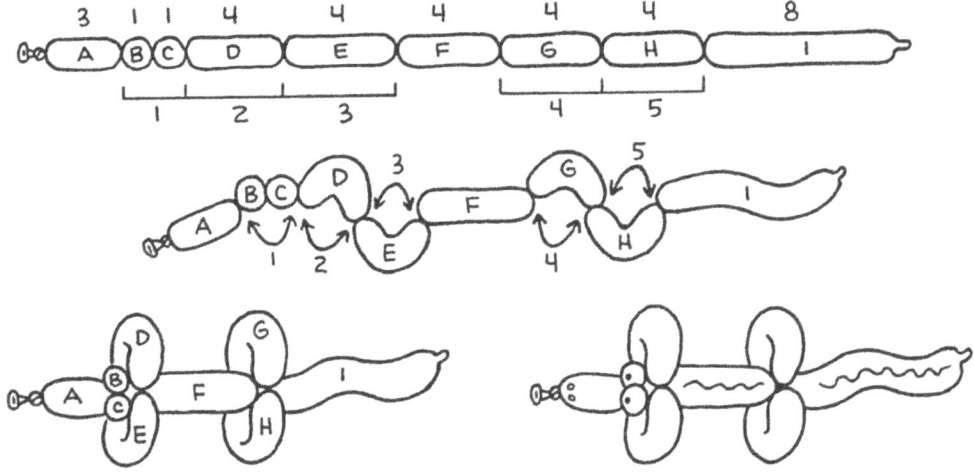

You can add character to the tail by bending it and squeezing in several spots to create a zigzag effect.

FLOWER

Flower designs use the fold twist for petals and leaves.

Inflate a 260, leaving about four inches of tail. Tie a knot.

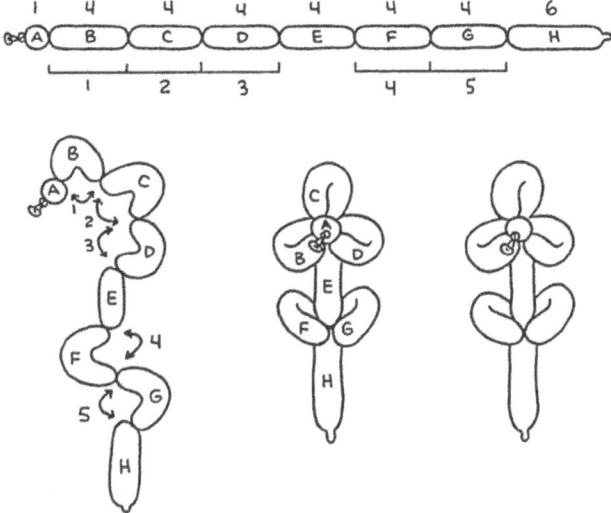

Flower designs seem to go over big with the girls. Boys get more excited over Swords. Notice that in this design the multiple fold twists are used to provide stability.

SWORD

Inflate a 260, leaving one to two inches of tail. Tie a knot.

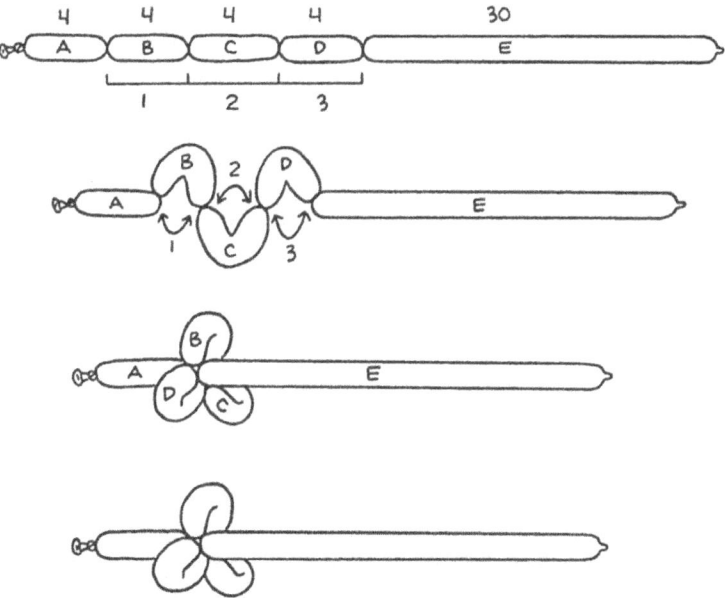

This design can be done with two or three fold twists.

BIRDS AND BEES

The looping forms of the fold twist can also be used to create wings for birds and bugs. The following diagram is two designs in one: a Hummingbird and a Bumblebee.

Inflate a 260, leaving about three inches of tail. Tie the knot.

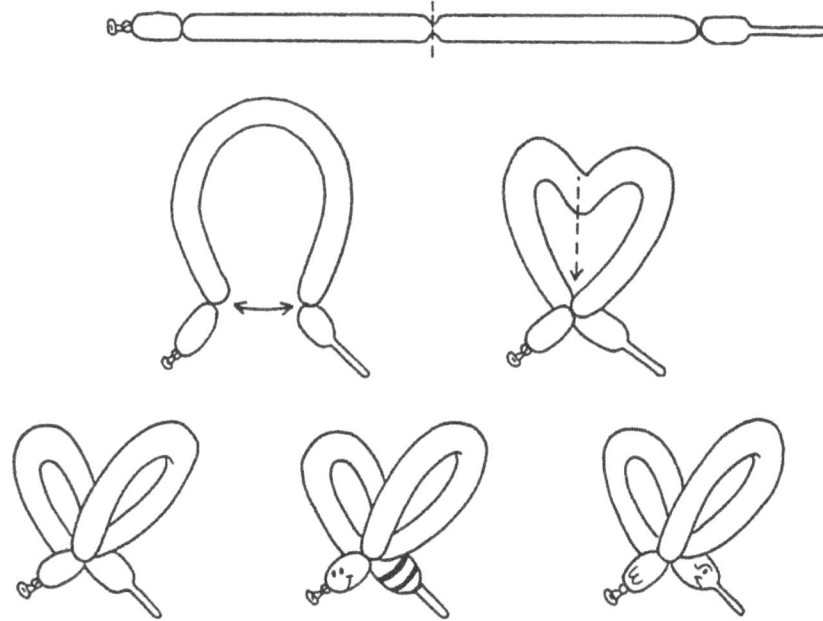

You can also make larger wings: Inflate a 260, leaving about one inch of tail. When you tie the knot, also tie the tail to the mouth of the balloon, creating a large loop. Attach this loop to a Bee Body balloon (shown in Chapter 1) for a big, impressive bee or bird.

Chapter Seven

Bears, Poodles, and Floppy-Eared Dogs

If I had to recommend one balloon animal that you must know how to make, it would be the Teddy Bear. This animal is cute, versatile, and challenging, and mastering it will make you appear to be an accomplished balloon artist. This design requires a lot of practice and a new twist, called an *ear twist*, which is actually a very small fold twist in disguise.

An ear twist is made of a small (one-inch) bubble that is twisted so that its two joints lock together. Unlike the fold twist, you must first create the bubble before locking the joints. Once the bubble is created, pull it so that its joints come closer together, then twist. The bubble will lock in place and look like a little crescent, resembling an ear. Most animals, of course, will have two of these. Though it is called an ear twist, this twist has many other design possibilities beyond ears, and you will use it often.

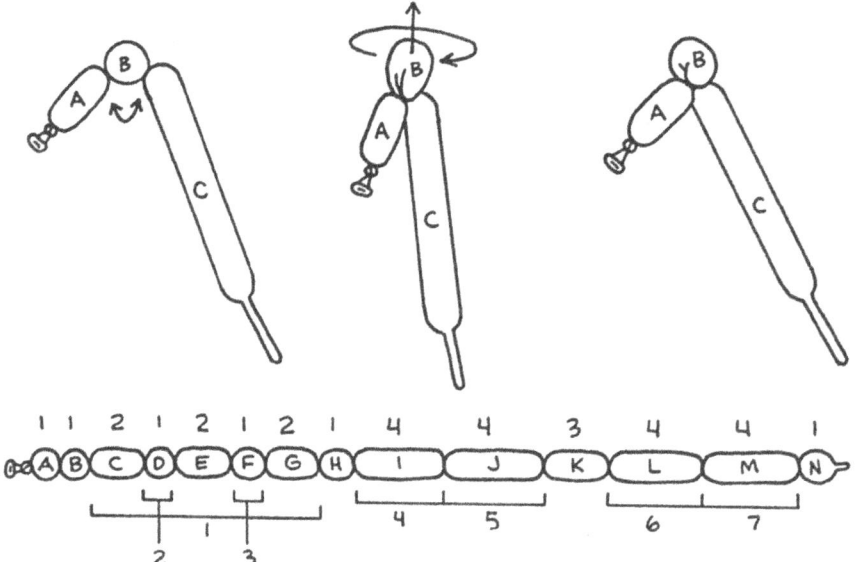

TEDDY BEAR

The Teddy Bear uses a lot of bubbles. You will make seven bubbles before you ever make your first lock twist, so remember to hold on to the first and last bubbles until they are locked. Because there are so many bubbles, you will need about five to six inches of tail after you inflate the balloon. Don't forget to tie the knot!

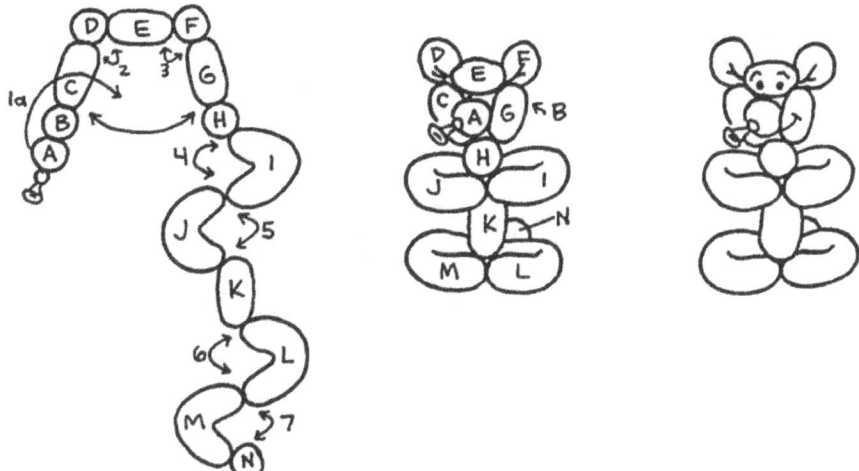

As I mentioned earlier, the Teddy Bear is versatile. He can be attached to other balloons with great ease by making one larger fold twist instead of two smaller ones for the arms and legs. Wrap the fold twist around another 260, then lock it in place. Your bear can now hang, sit, or swing on other designs.

POODLE

The Poodle design is based on the Basic Dog, but, as in real life, the Poodle is much fancier. Using more bubbles and a pom-pom, the Poodle design is always popular.

Inflate a 260, leaving about five inches of tail. Tie the knot.

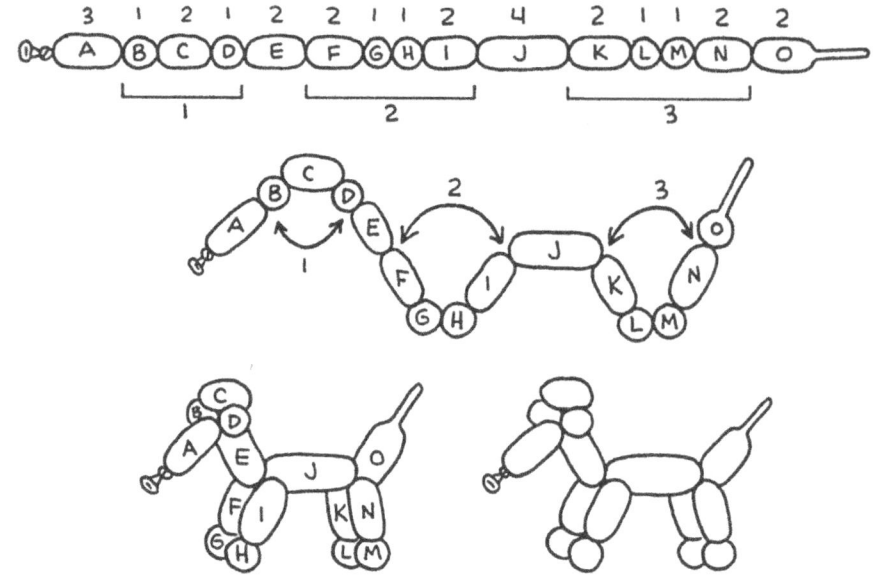

Once you have completed all of the twists in the design, prepare to make the pom-pom on the end of the tail. Hold the tip of the tail with one hand, exposing only about a quarter of an inch. With the other hand, grab the exposed portion of the tail, stretch it, and allow it to snap back. This weakens the tip of the tail. Continue to hold the tail, exposing just the tip. Squeeze the air that is in the base of the tail up into the tip, being careful to channel the air with your hand so that it can expand only into the tip of the tail. The tip will inflate. Release the balloon and your Poodle will have a pom-pom tail.

FLOPPY-EARED DOG

The Floppy-Eared Dog will show you another way to make ears on dogs. These ears look especially good on the Dachshund. The Floppy-Eared Dog can be designed sitting, which is also a good pose for Rabbits and Cats.

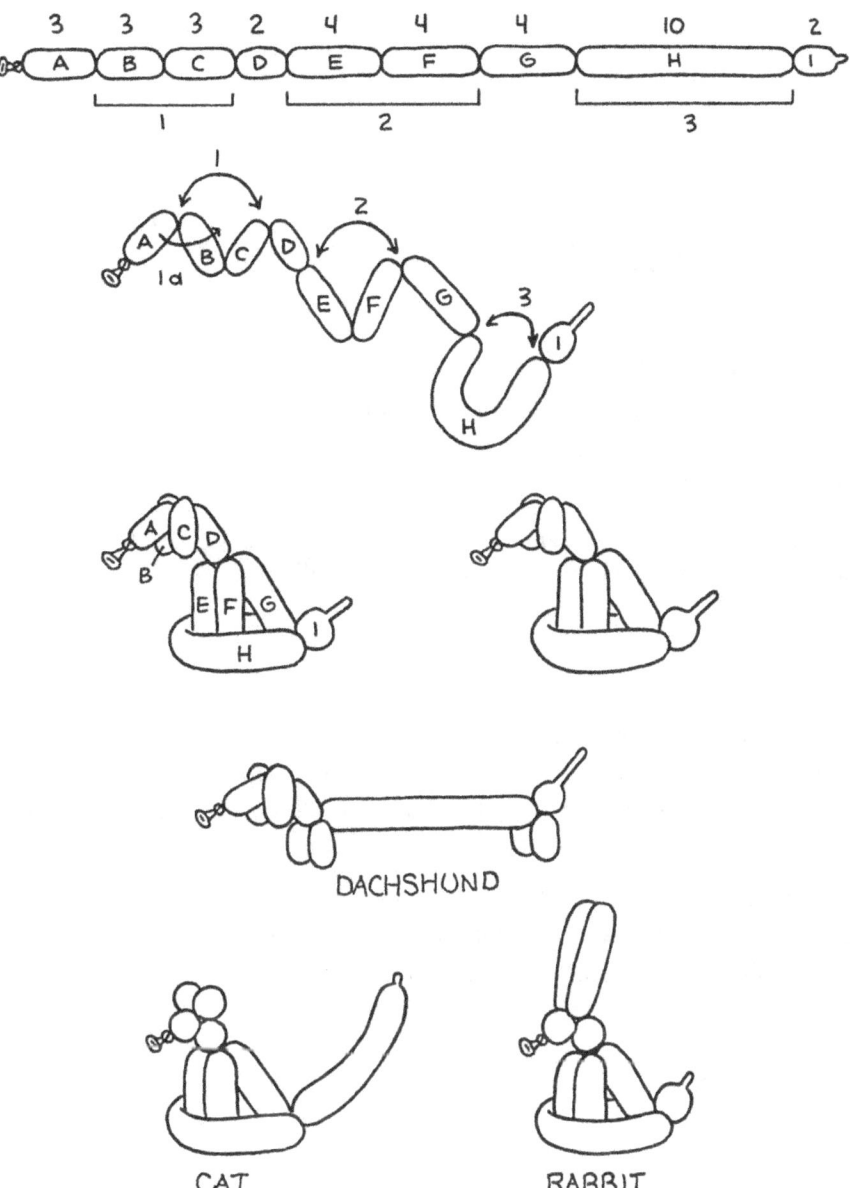

DACHSHUND

CAT

RABBIT

Chapter Eight

The Roll-Through

The *roll-through* is a twist that will give an extra dimension to your designs. It is most often used to add frill or body to a shape. All of the twists that we have worked with so far have aligned just one or two bubbles. The roll-through will allow us to align three bubbles or three chains of bubbles next to each other.

One of the simplest and loveliest designs that uses a roll-through is the Swan. Learn how to make a Swan and you will learn the basic fundamentals for a roll-through!

SWAN

Inflate a 260, leaving about three to four inches of tail. Tie the knot. The beginning of the design actually resembles the head and ears of the Rabbit design. Make one small bubble about two to three inches in length, then make two longer bubbles about six to seven inches long. Lock twist them as shown. This will be the tail and wings of the Swan.

The next bubble will be the same length as the two previous bubbles. Tilt it back so that it lies in the crease formed by those two bubbles, then begin to press it through that crease, rolling the other two bubbles to help force it through. Its joints will be locked in place at both ends of this roll-through formation.

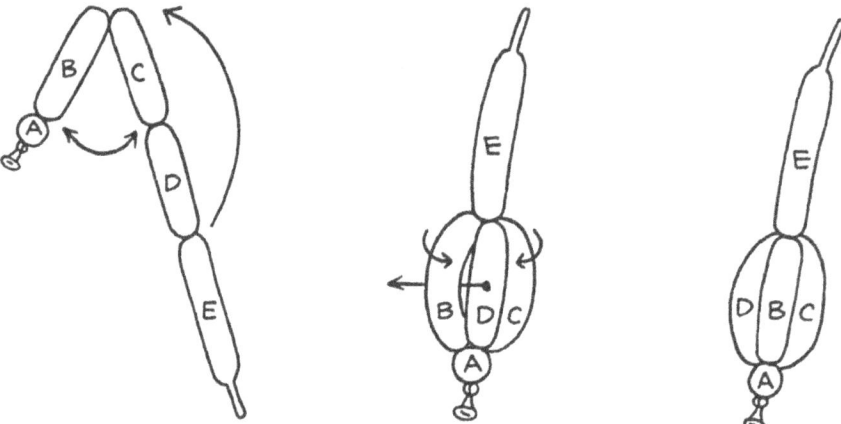

Once the roll-through is formed, the rest of the balloon is brought back and tucked between two of the three bubbles in the roll-through. This is the neck of the Swan. Wrap this long bubble around your hand and squeeze it gently, allowing it to form the graceful curve of a swan's neck. The remaining portion of the tail should be about two inches long. This will be the bill of your Swan. Pull it down toward the body of the Swan to give it more character.

Note how the roll-through is presented in the following diagram of the Swan so that you will understand how to read it in future diagrams.

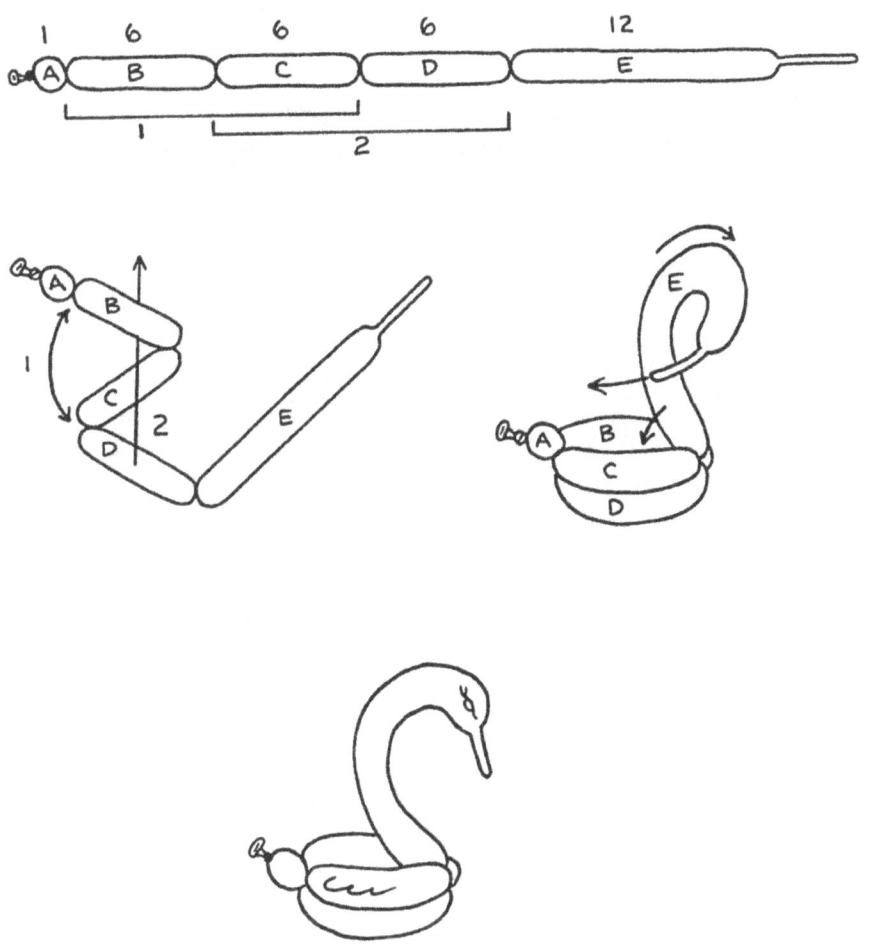

STEGOSAURUS

Roll-throughs can be created with chains of bubbles and can be used to suggest hair, legs, or scales like the ones on the back of this dinosaur! It is important that you twist each bubble in the chain several times so that they will not come undone when rolled through.

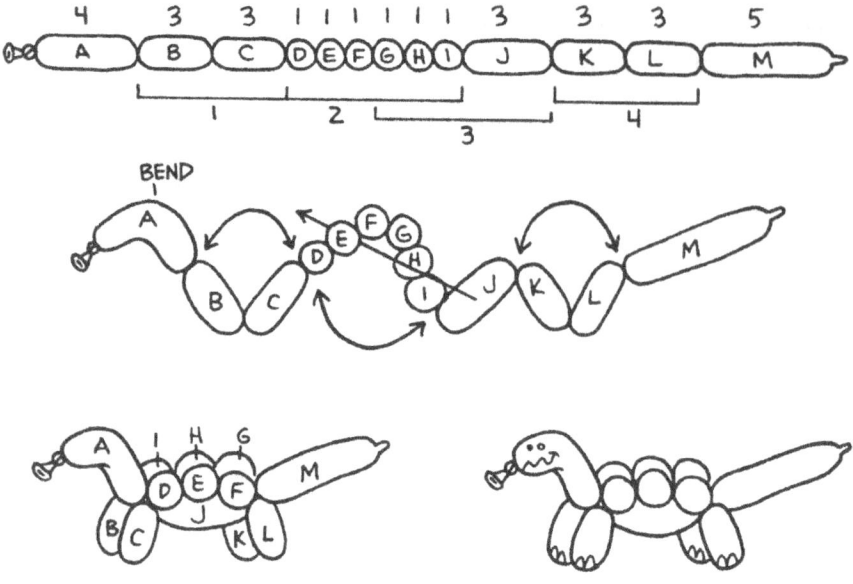

DETAILED HORSE

This same technique can be added to the Basic Horse to create a mane. Add a few extra bubbles on the legs to give the impression of hooves and the Horse becomes a much more interesting design.

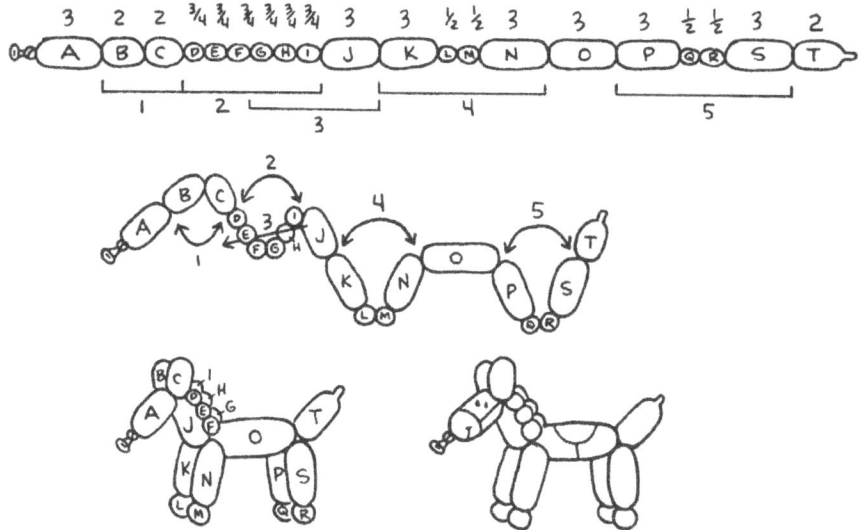

Later in this book the roll-through will become an important element of some of the bigger designs because it can create shapes with volume. Using the roll-through, sphere shapes for heads and oval shapes for bodies can easily be made. These shapes can also be used in smaller designs, as we will see in the following Rubber Ducky design. Carefully note how changes in the length of bubbles used in a roll-through will change the shape.

RUBBER DUCKY

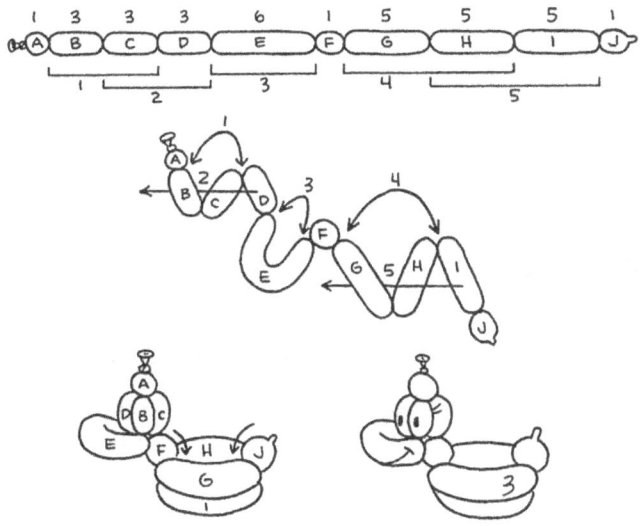

TURTLE OR LADYBUG

The following is the teeniest roll-through design, and it makes a cute bracelet. It can become two designs if you change the color of the balloon used. Green makes a Turtle and red makes a Ladybug! (To create the bracelet, just wrap the uninflated end several times around bubble A.)

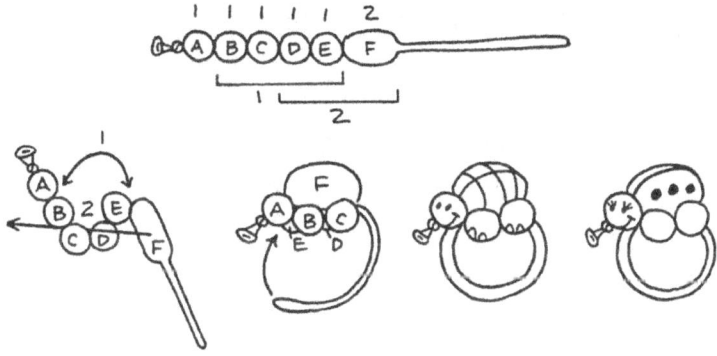

Chapter Nine

Unusual Twists

All of the twists that you have learned so far are very fundamental, and you will use them continually as you develop your skills. The following twists, however, are a bit more specialized. They are more difficult to do but will open a whole new area of creative possibilities.

THE TULIP TWIST

The *tulip twist* is so named because it is used to make a bubble that looks like the cup of a tulip.

To make a tulip twist, inflate a 260 and tie the knot. Use your index finger to press the knot into the body of the balloon. While your finger is in the balloon, use the thumb and index finger of your other hand to pinch the body of the balloon and grasp the knot inside. Remove your index finger from inside the bubble, continuing to grasp the knot with your other hand. Twist the newly formed bubble, locking the knot inside the body of the balloon.

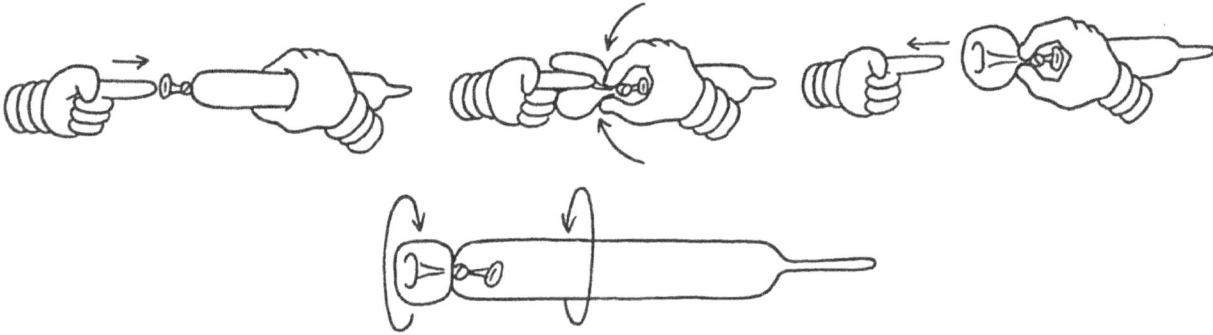

When it is part of the design, the tulip twist will always be the first bubble you make, and will be noted on the bubble diagram as ⊙.

TULIP

To make an actual tulip balloon, inflate a 260 so that there is just enough air for one bubble. When you press the knot in, press it into the tail of the balloon. Once the knot is locked, press it back into the bubble, securing it in place. The result is a whimsical tulip. Try making several of them and tucking them into the arm of a Teddy Bear design.

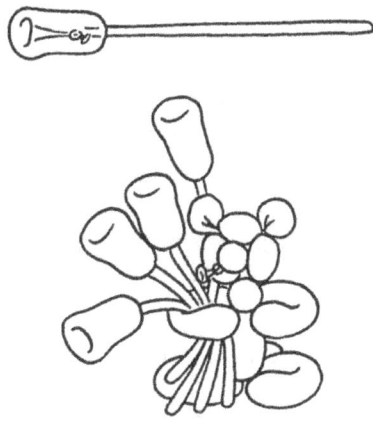

PIG

The tulip twist can be used to make a cute nose that transforms a bear's head into a pig's head.

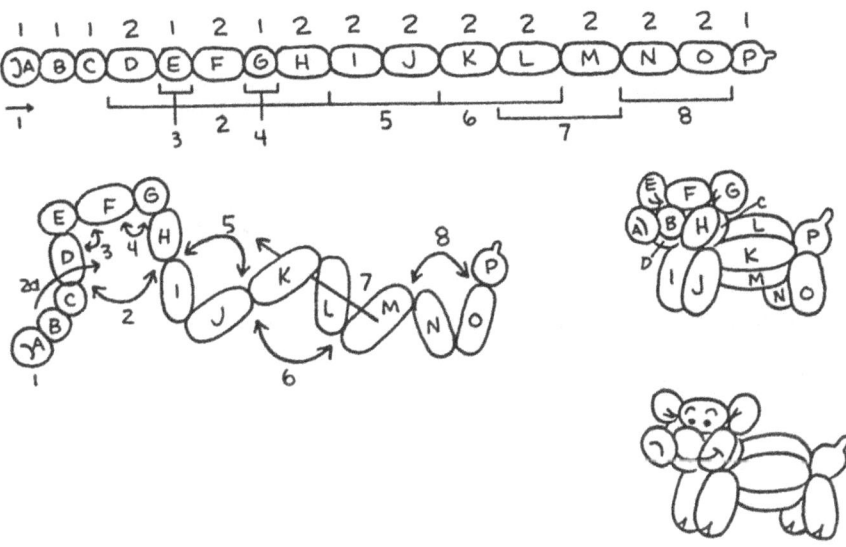

INSERTS OR SEEDS

It is possible to insert a small bubble into the body of a 260 and have it bob freely inside your finished design. This makes for almost magical designs that are a lot of fun to play with.

Inflate a 260 and tie the knot. Make a bubble that is smaller than the width of the balloon's body. Press the small bubble into the body of the balloon with your index finger. Grasp the bubble, then pinch above the knot with the index finger and thumb of your other hand.

Continue to hold the bubble and remove your finger from inside the balloon, using your fingernail to tear the inserted bubble loose. Allow the bubble to fall into the body of the balloon. Continue to grasp the torn end of the balloon and tie a knot.

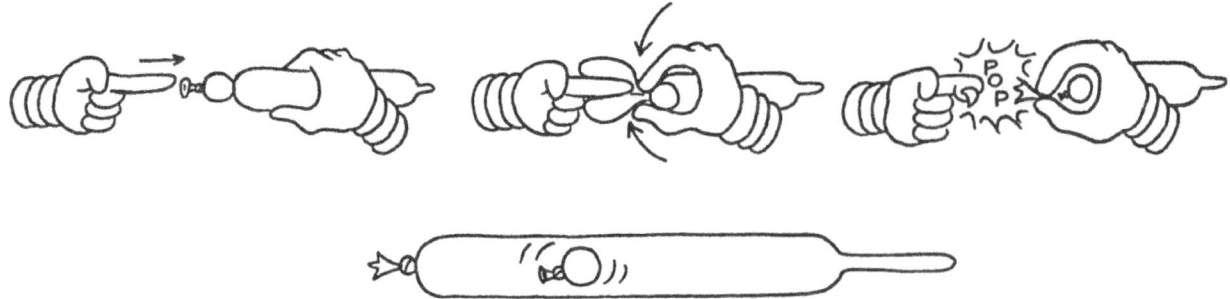

This may take some practice, but the effect is worth it.

Once the bubble is inside, you can make any design you wish, trapping the floating bubble in any bubble of the design. Shown here is a bubble in a dog's belly.

HOT DOG WITH A MEATBALL INSIDE (AKA PREGNANT PUP)

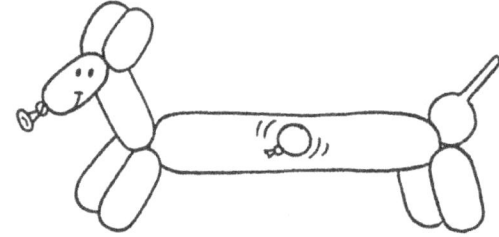

SPLIT TWISTS AND POP TWISTS

These two twists give you the opportunity to create some very fancy and challenging designs that will impress anyone.

A split twist begins its life as an ear twist. Once you have formed an ear twist, divide or "split" that bubble into two smaller bubbles by carefully twisting the ear twist in half using the joint that is its base as the dividing line. Twist these two smaller bubbles at their base to more firmly lock them in place.

The split twist by itself can be used like a hinge allowing you to change the direction of the balloon as shown. This technique can be used to make letters and numbers!

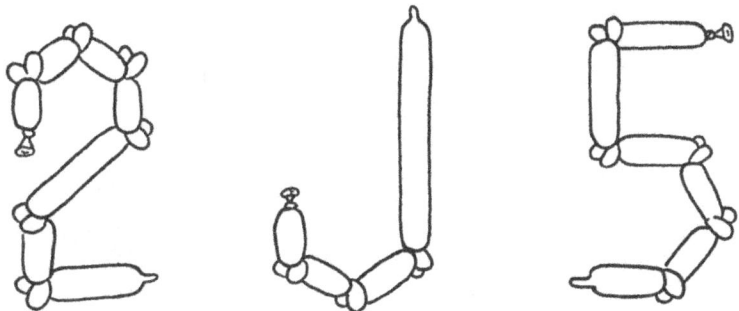

The pop twist incorporates the split twist, allowing you to make arms and legs that are independent of each other. Other applications are wings on airplanes and handlebars for motorcycles, to name a few.

The pop twist consists of a chain of bubbles that lock together to create a loop. The center bubble between two split twists is broken or "popped" to divide the chain into two branches of bubbles. The split twists secure the air in the bubbles that had been connected to the popped bubble.

Do not attempt to pop the bubble in the pop twist by biting it! Use your fingernail, keys, or some other instrument.

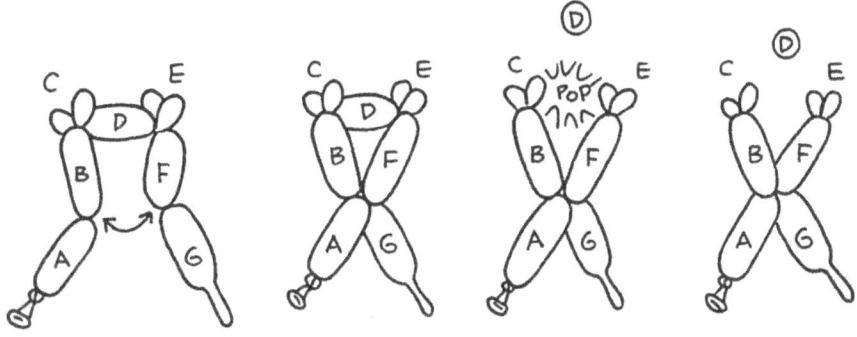

MONKEY

The Monkey is a fun animal application of the pop twist, which is used to form arms and legs.

Inflate a 260, leaving at least six to seven inches of tail. Tie the knot.

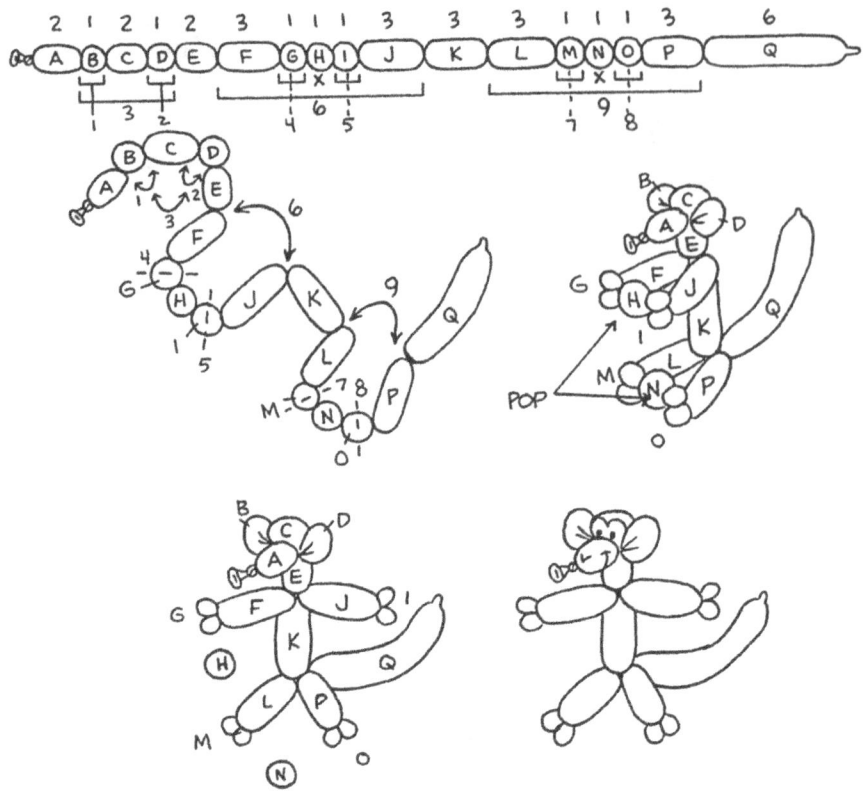

AIRPLANE

The Airplane, like the Monkey design, requires two sets of pop twists. They form the tail and wings of this balloon jetliner.

Inflate a 260, leaving about four inches of tail. Tie the knot.

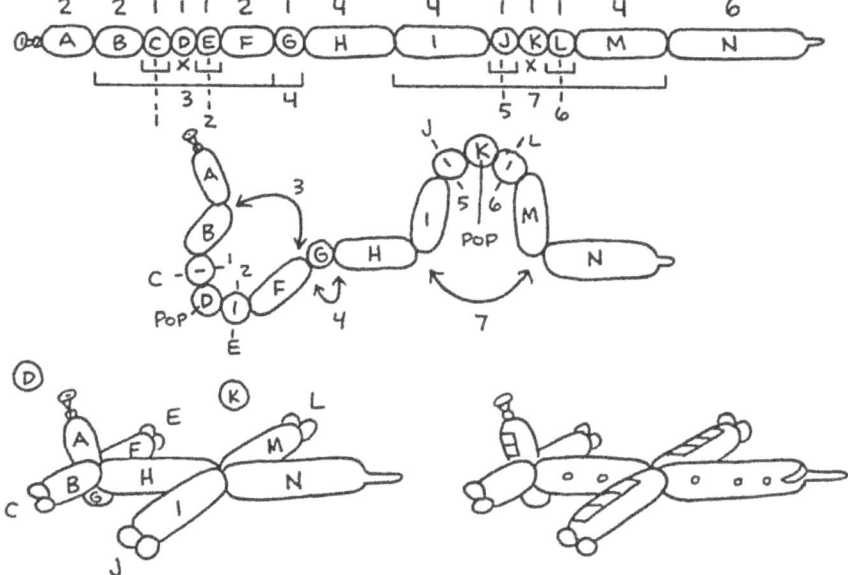

MOTORCYCLE

The Motorcycle design has only one pop twist, which forms the handlebars. Carefully note how the wheels are made by tucking bubbles into the center of a fold twist.

Inflate a 260, leaving about five inches of tail. Tie the knot.

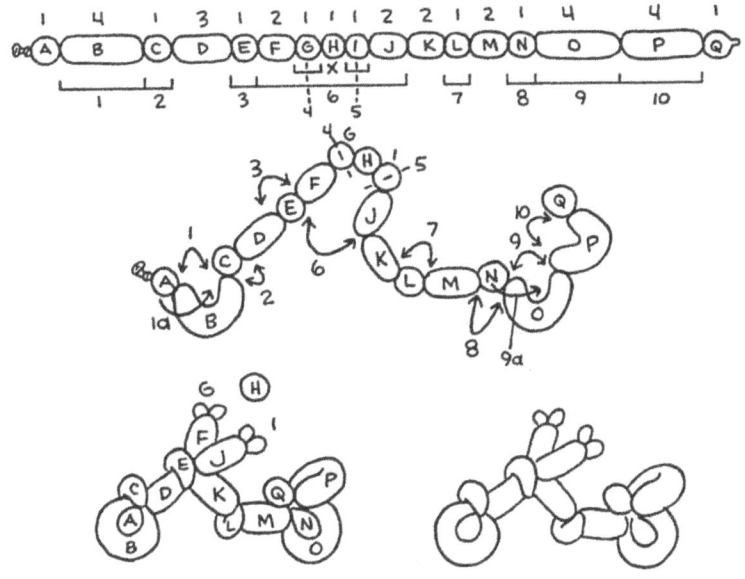

SPIRAL

The spiral is a lot of fun, and it requires no twisting! It does help to weaken the balloon, however, so before you begin, inflate a 260 all the way, then release the air. Your balloon will now be easier to inflate and will be a bit longer.

Grasp the tip of the balloon between the base of your index and middle finger and wrap the rest of the balloon around both fingers. Be careful not to overlap or twist the balloon; it must lie flat. Inflate the balloon, making sure that it inflates around your fingers into a nice tight spiral.

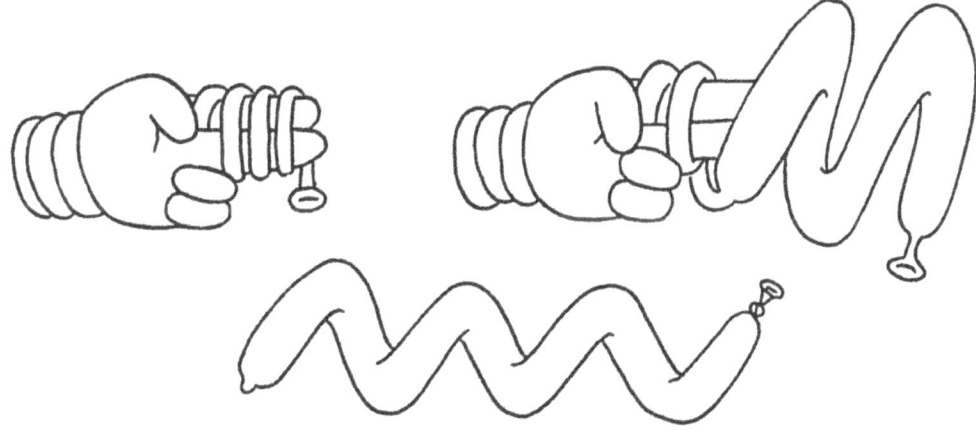

COBRA

The Cobra is a great design that is made easily with the spiral. First create a spiral, then make the two bubbles and fold twist that form the head.

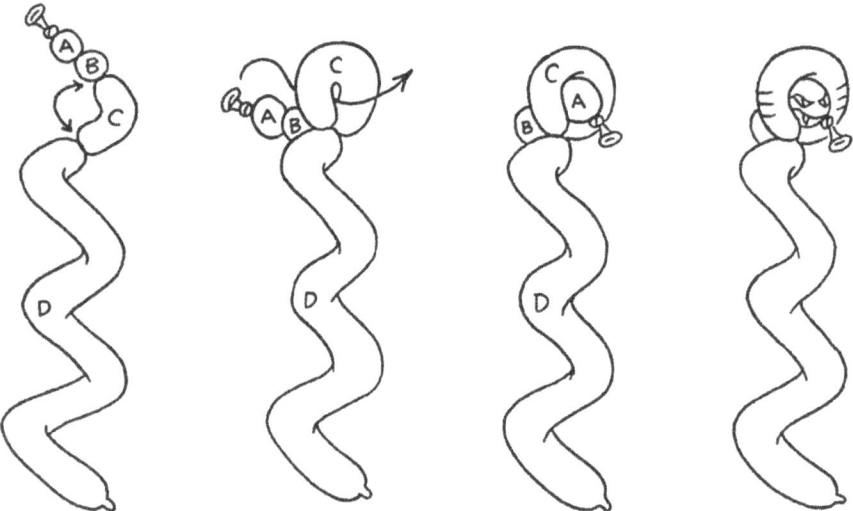

Chapter Ten

Hats

The balloon hat is a great way to have your work as a balloon artist get noticed. Hats are usually bigger designs and sit up high where everyone can see them. The best thing about balloon hats is that they are simple and fast to make. It is easy to be creative with balloon hats. You can add balloons just about anywhere on a balloon hat and it will look interesting.

The following designs are basic, with a few suggestions on how to get crazy. Experiment! Add designs that you already know and make up new ones. Balloon hats, above all, should be fun and crazy!

HEADBAND

The most basic hat is the Headband. It converts easily into a Feather Headdress, Daniel Boone Hat, Flapper Hat, or a Pilot's Headset!

Inflate a 260, leaving about an inch of tail. Tie the knot.

Wrap the balloon around the wearer's head for that custom fit and lock as shown, creating a loop with two tails of balloon that are about the same length. This Headband is perfect for ninjas, warriors, and flower children!

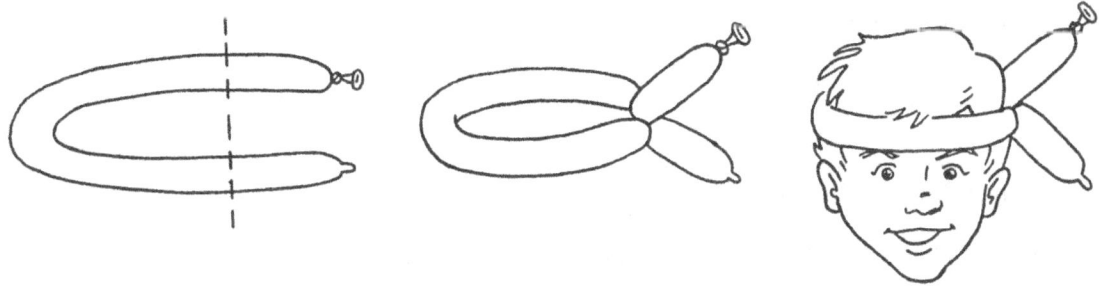

To transform the Headband into the other designs that were mentioned, make a few minor changes.

Inflate a 260, leaving about two inches of tail instead of one inch. Tie the knot.

Begin the hat with a one-inch bubble, then make the loop and lock in place. Make a pom-pom on the end of the tail as was described in the Poodle design. How you position the hat on the wearer's head will determine what the hat is, as shown in the following illustrations.

To eliminate the tail for the Feather Headdress and Daniel Boone hat, leave only an inch of tail when you inflate the 260.

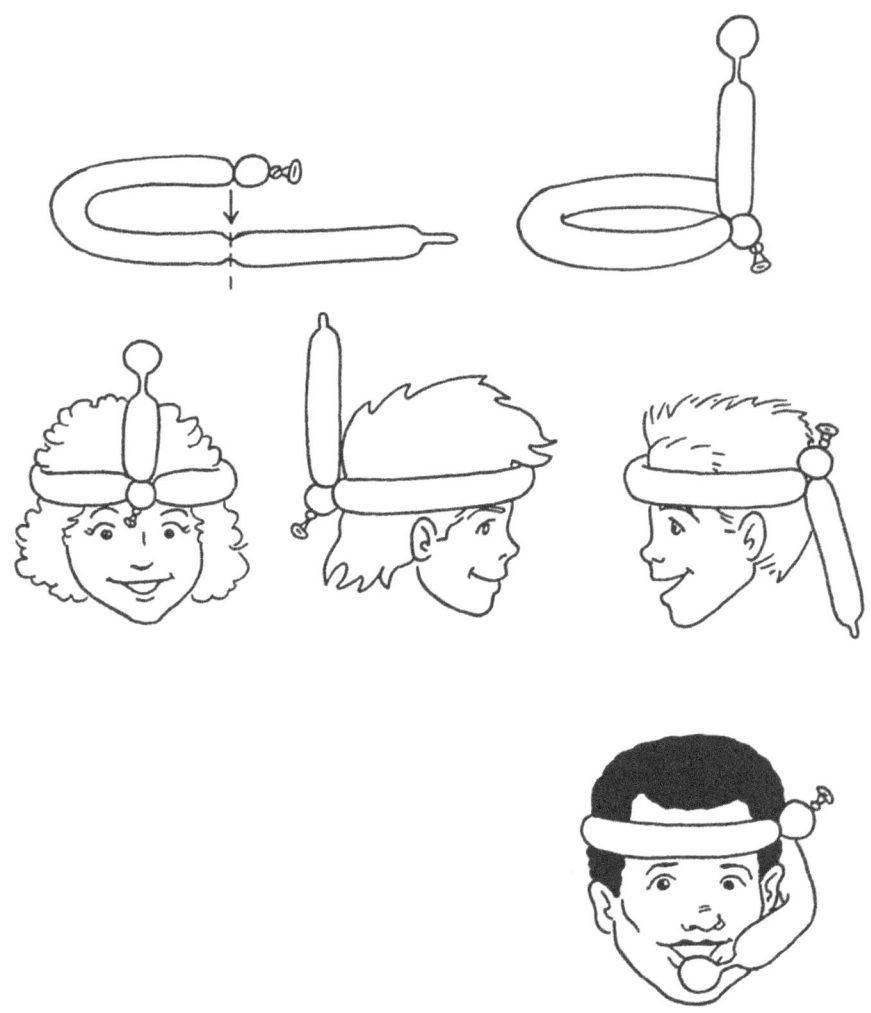

The Pilot's Headset requires a bend to be squeezed into the balloon to change its direction, allowing it to hang in front of the wearer's mouth like a microphone. (Sometimes warming the balloon up by rubbing it against your shirt or leg helps to make it bend.)

SPACE HELMET

The Space Helmet is an important hat to learn because it acts as a foundation to add other balloons onto. The Space Helmet begins with a one-inch bubble, like most of the other designs. After the loop is made, the remaining portion of the balloon is brought over the top of the loop and locked as shown. You can add a pom-pom for an antenna by allowing enough tail in your balloon before you start.

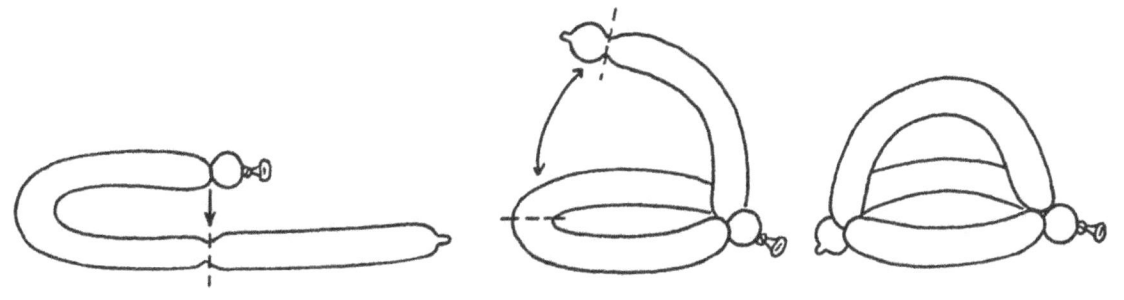

SPACE HELMET WITH POM-POM

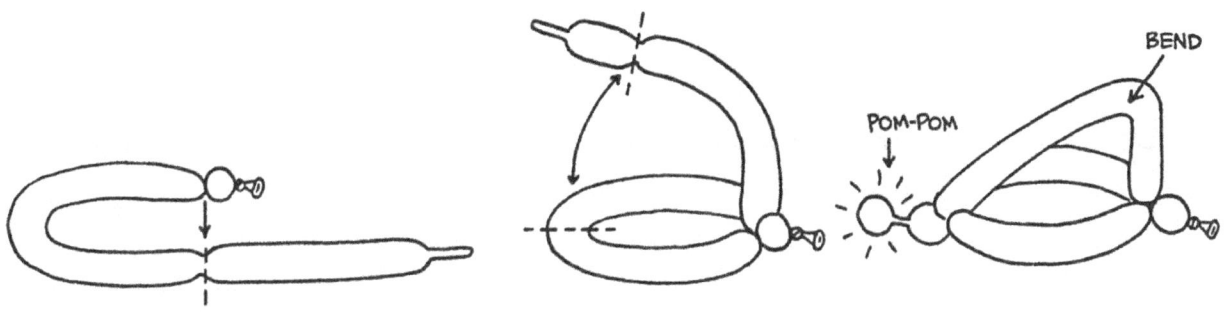

WILD ANTENNAE

Now that you know how to make a Space Helmet, you can add balloons and get crazier. Inflate a 260 all the way. Fold it in half and attach it to the helmet as shown.

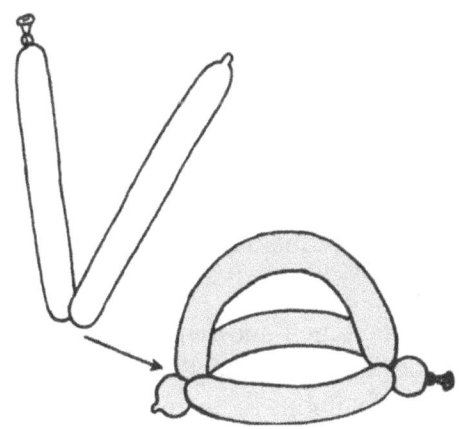

or

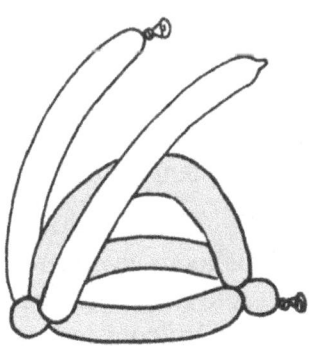

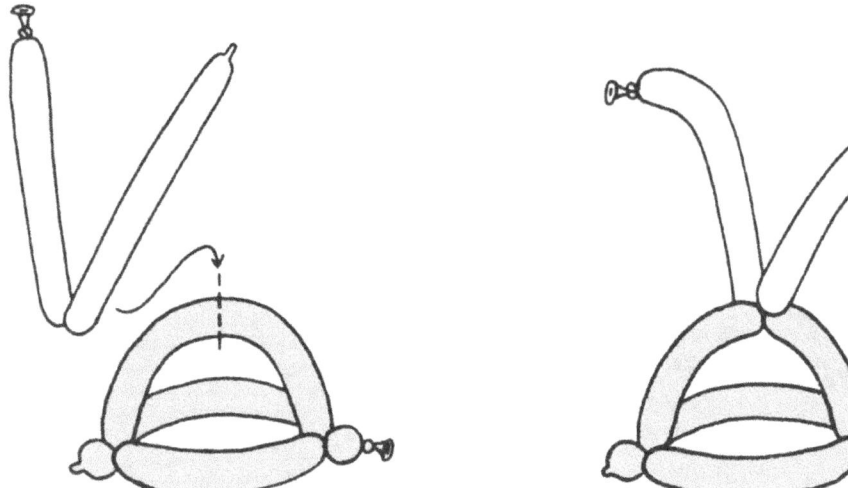

You can bring the ends of the added balloon down and attach as shown below to make wings.

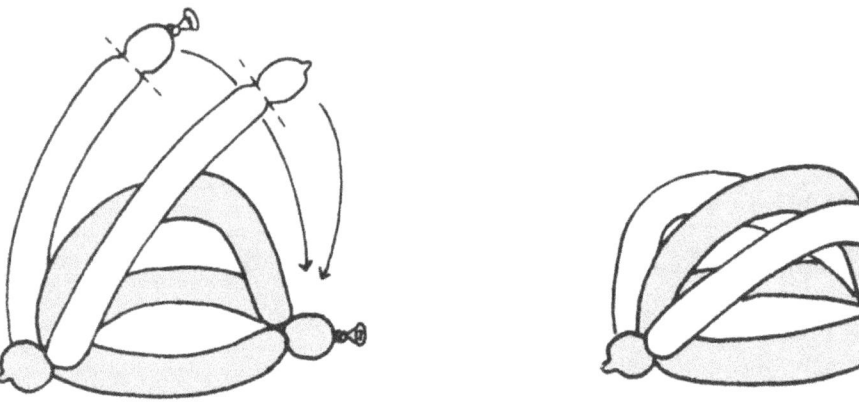

HAIRY HATS

You can make hats that look like they have wild hair by adding two 260s to the basic helmet as shown. You will soon begin to see how much fun you can have making hats just by adding balloons.

You can lock balloons anywhere on the helmet by using the pinch-and-twist method that is used when making fold twists. Align balloons at the joints you wish to connect, squeeze gently, and twist, locking the balloons in place. Always check that the balloons to be connected in this manner are not overinflated, or they will be likely to burst while you are twisting.

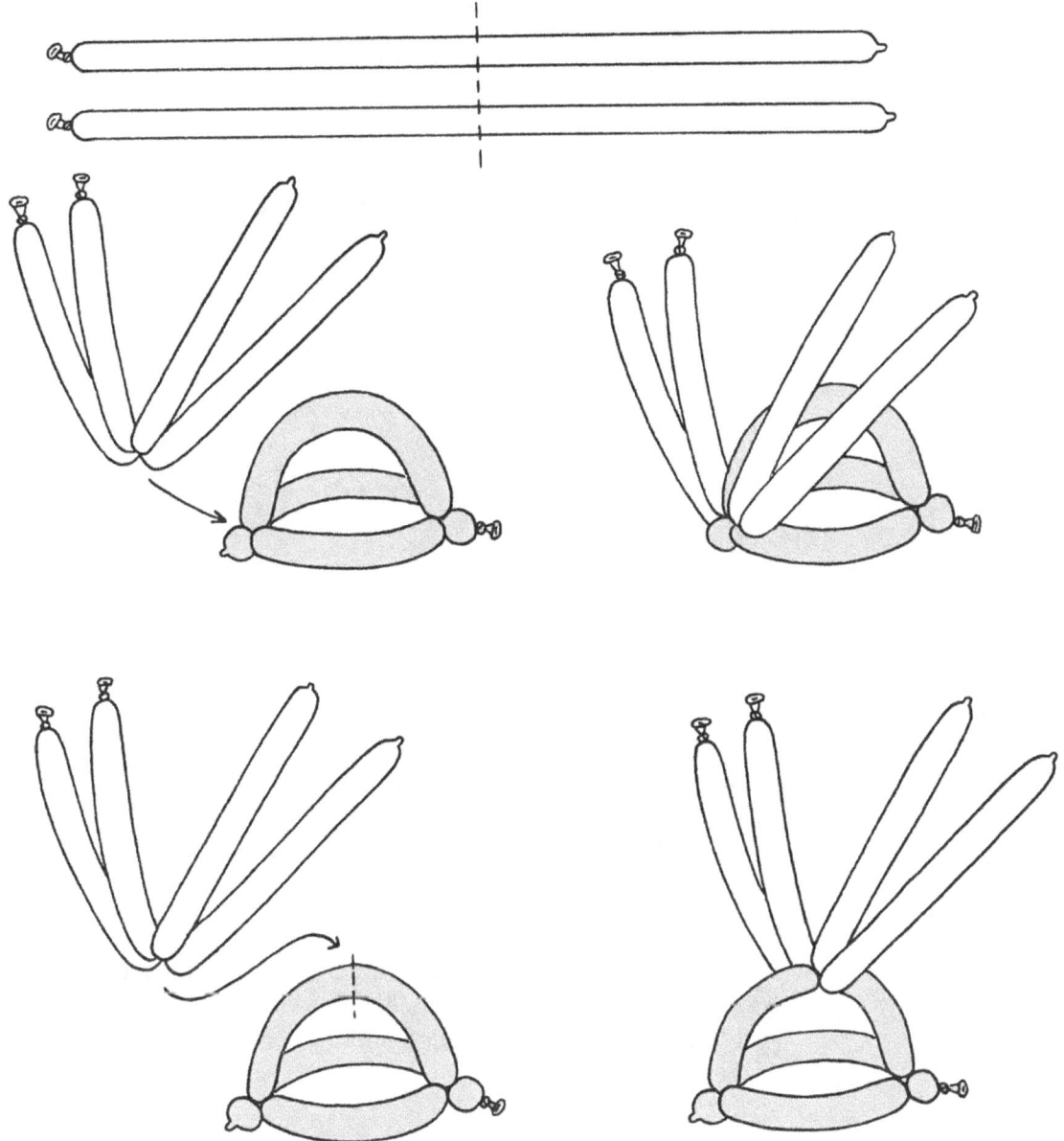

Try connecting the ends of the bubbles that make the hair on the Hairy Hats. One will look like a bike helmet, and the other begins to look like a crown.

BIKE HELMET

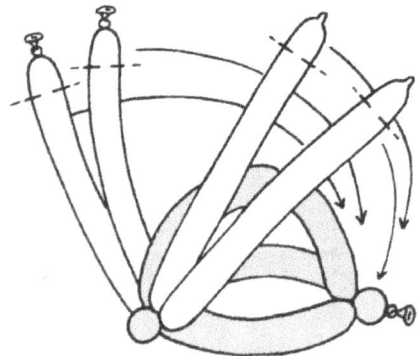 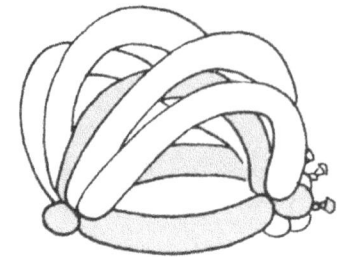

CROWN

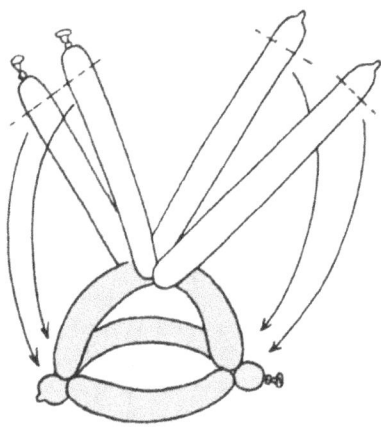 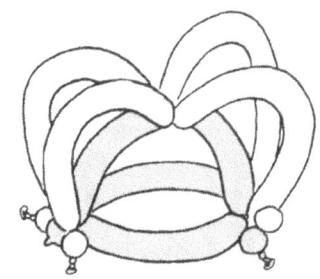

You can cap the Crown off with a small round balloon for a King's Crown or a six-inch heart balloon for a Queen's Crown. Just wrap the knot of the added balloon around the joint at the top of the hat.

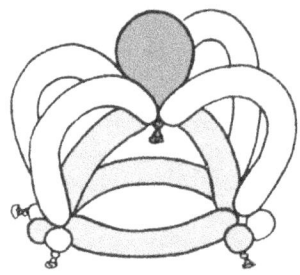 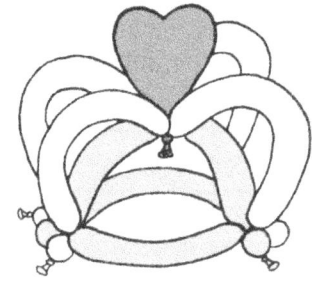

The Crown is a very sturdy base to add other balloons onto. Using this base, you can create towering hats that are as stable as the head that is wearing them. The following is a hat that I like to make for birthday kids. I like to call it a Super-Duper Hat!

SUPER-DUPER HAT

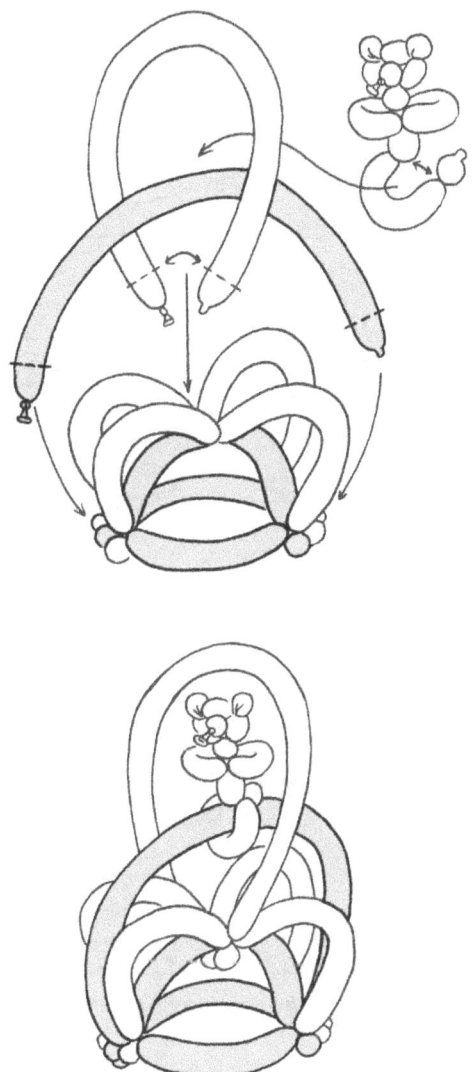

Another way of creating a hat is by making twists or braids with 260s and connecting them at the ends to form headbands. The twists and braids themselves make great balloon designs even when they are not used as hats. (For example, a red and green braid makes a nice Christmas wreath.)

TWIST HAT

Begin with two 260s. Inflate them both, leaving about two inches of tail. Tie each knot. Lock twist the two balloons together at the bottom. Starting at that point, twist the balloons upward so that they wrap around each other as shown. Holding both ends of the wrapped balloons, measure the wearer's head. Lock the ends of the twist together, forming a band.

Depending on the size of the wearer's head, there should be a fair amount of each balloon left over with tails. Add pom-poms to these for added effect!

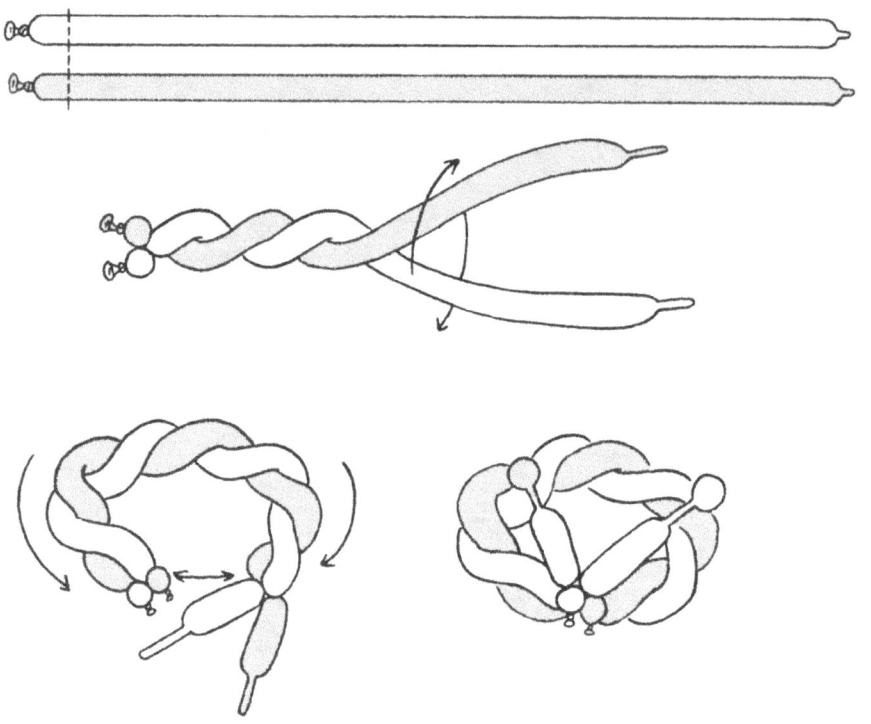

BRAIDED HAT (ALADDIN'S TURBAN)

The braid begins the same way the twist did, except that three 260s are joined at the bottom instead of two. They will be labeled balloons A, B, and C.

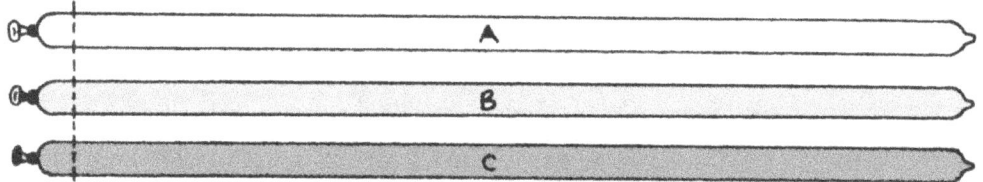

Balloon A will cross over balloon B and remain between B and C.

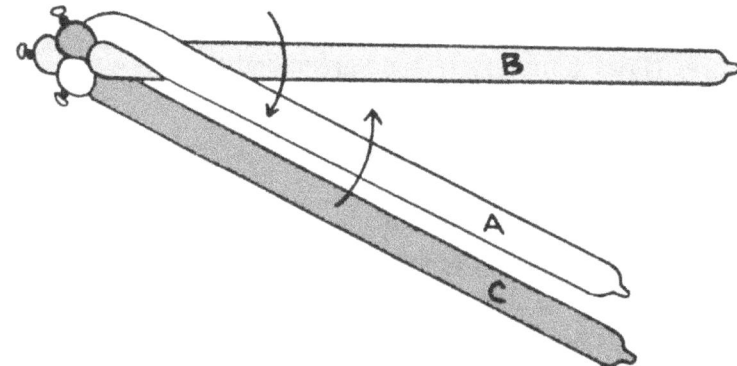

C will cross back over A and remain between B and A.

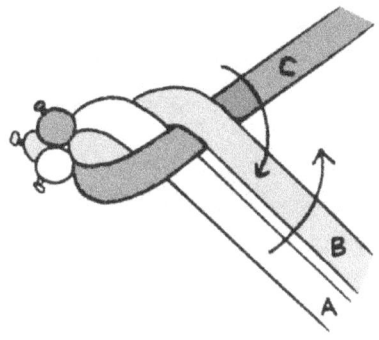

B will cross over C and remain between C and A.

Continue braiding in this order until you are beginning to run out of room. Measure the wearer's head and lock all three bubbles together at the end.

PRINCESS HAT

A hat that is one of my favorites is the Princess Hat. It requires only two balloons, one 260 fully inflated (be sure to give it a good burp!) and one inflated six-inch heart.

The headband is made differently than those previously shown. Follow the diagram, making the twists after you have measured the wearer's head.

There is truly no end to how creative you can get while making balloon hats. I have entertained in large rooms full of people and made no two hats the same. The following are some sample ideas for hats that are all made by combining balloon design elements that you are learning in this book.

LIGHTNING BOLT HAT

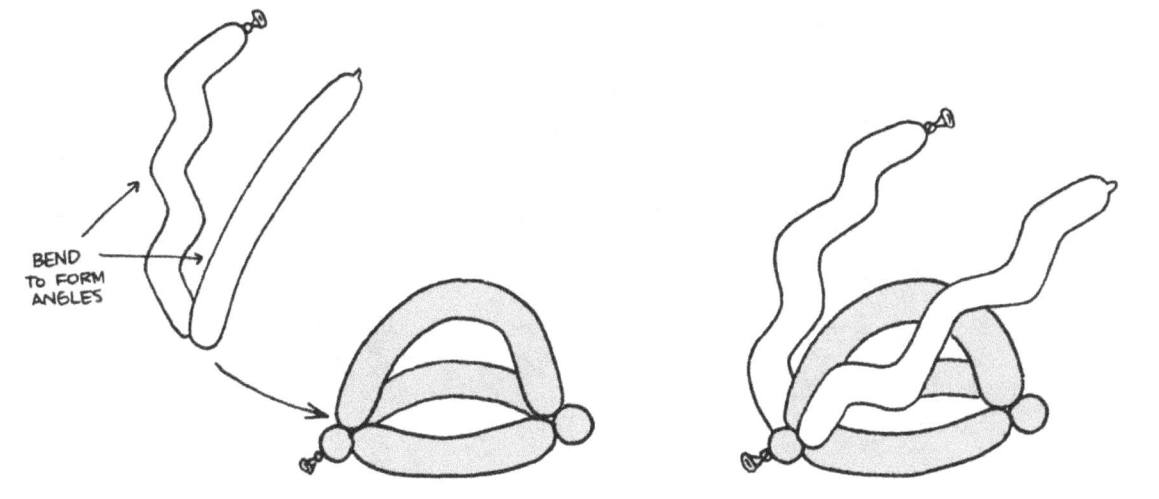

FLOWER HAT

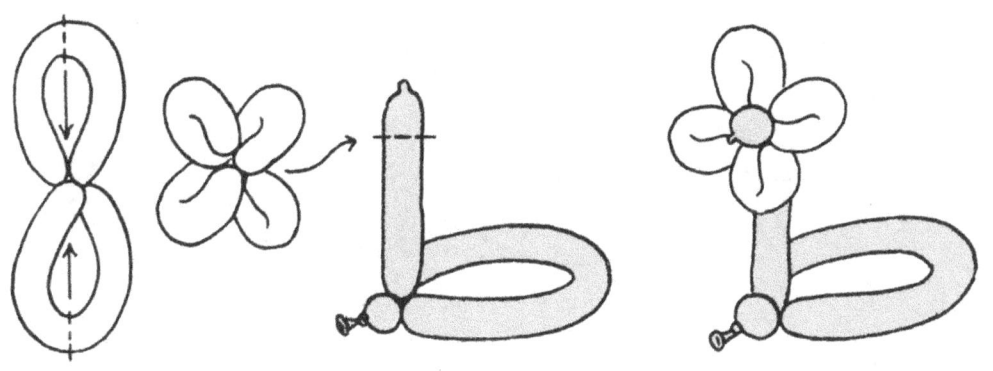

SPIRAL HAT

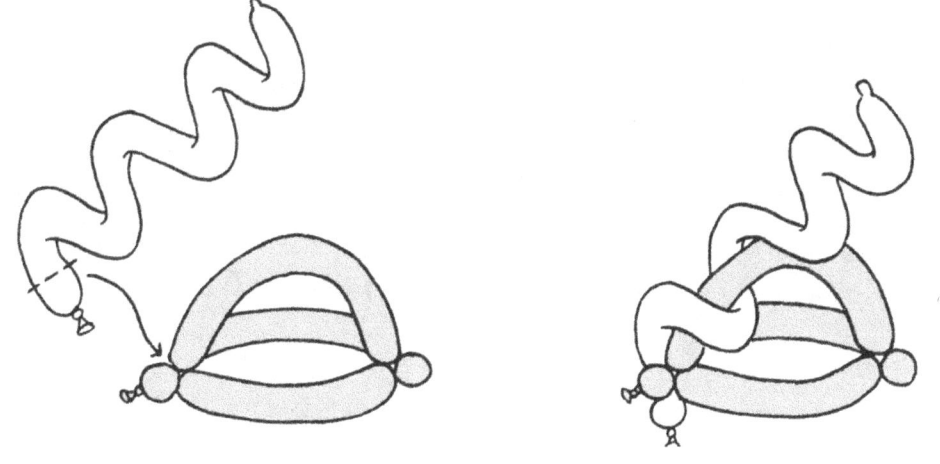

SUPER SPACE HAT

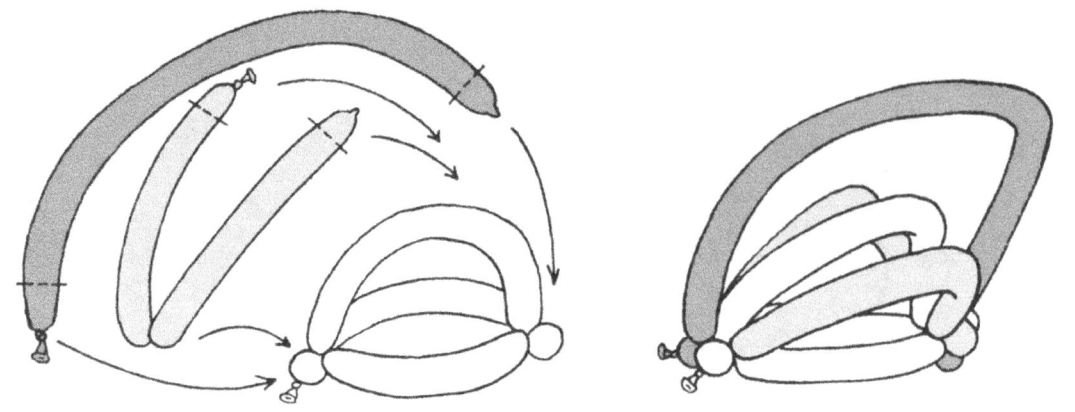

MOUSE EARS

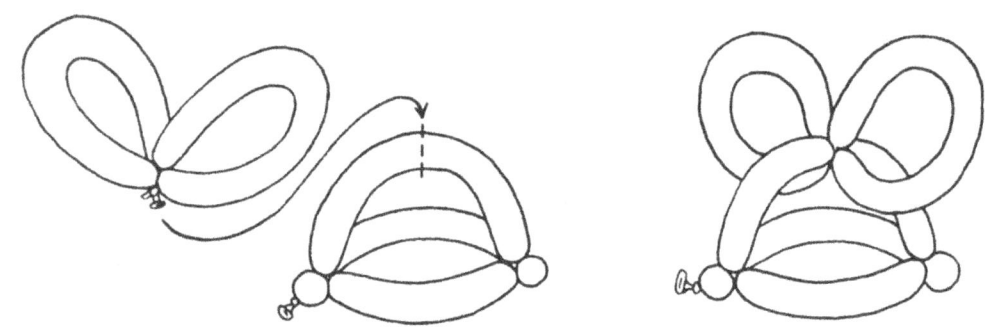

OCTOPUS HAT

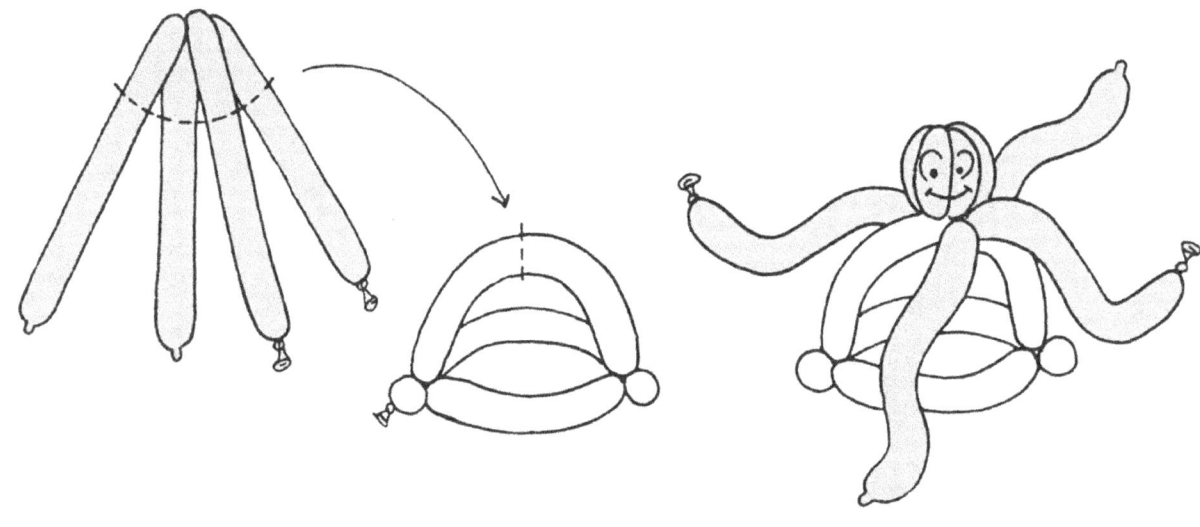

MONKEY IN A TREE HAT

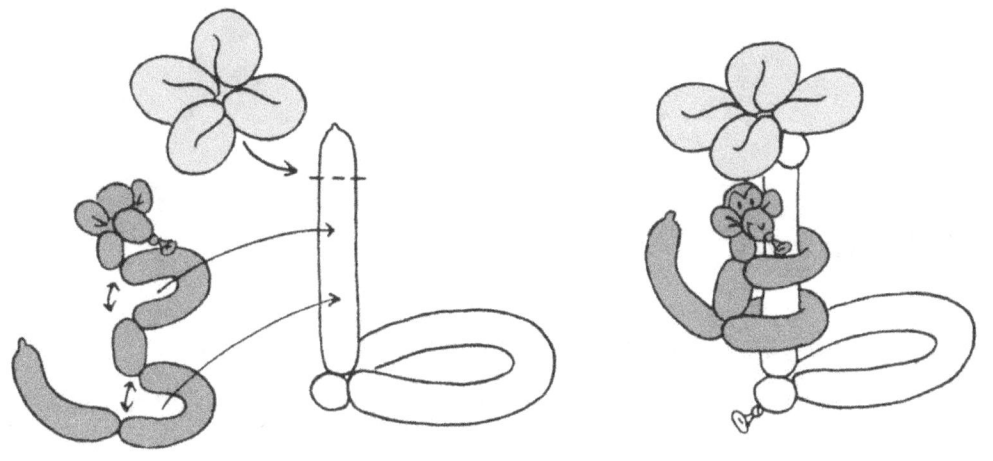

SPARTAN HAT

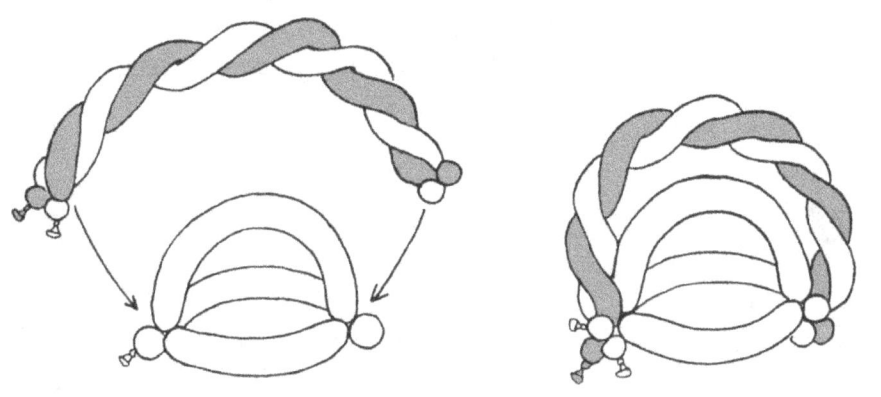

HEART HAT

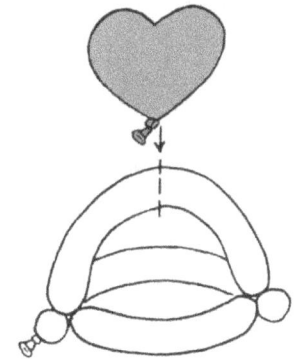

Chapter Eleven

Heart Designs

The most popular shape that you will ever use when making balloon designs has to be the heart shape. Oohs and aahs are almost always heard when a balloon artist uses a heart-shaped balloon in a balloon sculpture or makes a heart shape out of a 260.

The best news is that heart shapes are very quick to make. The six-inch heart balloon comes "ready-made," inflates quickly, and forms an instant and perfect heart shape. Making a heart out of a 260 requires only making a loop and giving it a squeeze in the right spot. Both are attractive and can be easily incorporated into many designs. They are great when used with animal designs, especially the Teddy Bear, and are wonderful for dressing up balloon hats!

As I mentioned, it is easy to make a heart shape out of a 260, but its simplicity may seem overstated until you learn and have practiced the skills required. Balloon artists have developed several ways to form heart shapes with 260s. I personally have had the most success with the technique that is illustrated below.

First you must create a loop with the 260. This is done by inflating the balloon fully and either locking or tying the ends of the balloon together. When tying the ends, you may wish to allow a little bit of tail to work with. Tying the ends eliminates the need to tie the knot in the balloon after inflation. You may have a preference, but you will find that each technique has certain applications that it is more appropriate for, so learn to work with both.

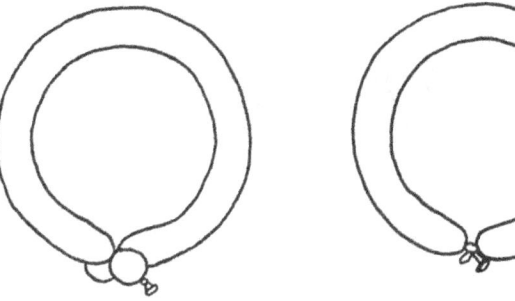

Once you have made the loop, find the top of it and pull it down to meet the point where the ends join. Grasp the folded portion of the balloon with both hands and gently squeeze out all of the air and hold for a moment, allowing the warmth from your hands to help form the shape. Slowly release the balloon, making sure that it does not pop out of your hands. The loop now transforms into the outline of a heart shape.

Practice this technique until you are happy with your heart shapes.

Once the heart shape is made, you can add other creations to it. A lovely and popular addition is the Lovebirds on a Heart design.

LOVEBIRDS ON A HEART

Inflate a 260, leaving about three inches of tail. Tie the knot.

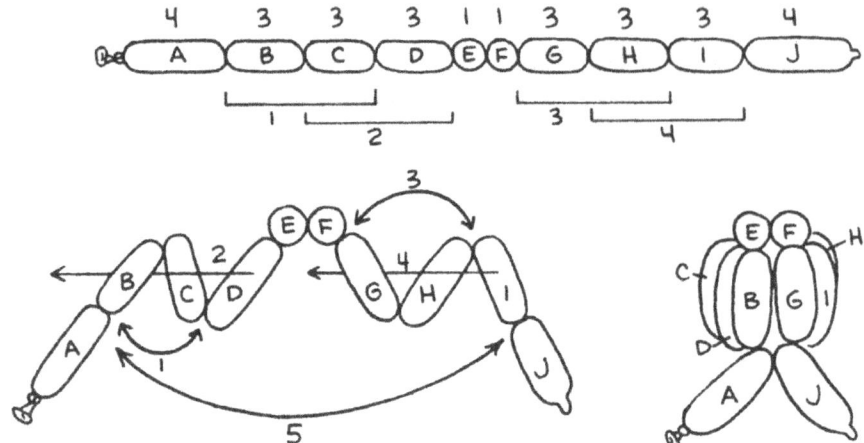

Attach to the heart shape as shown. This attaches best when the ends of the heart are tied together instead of locked.

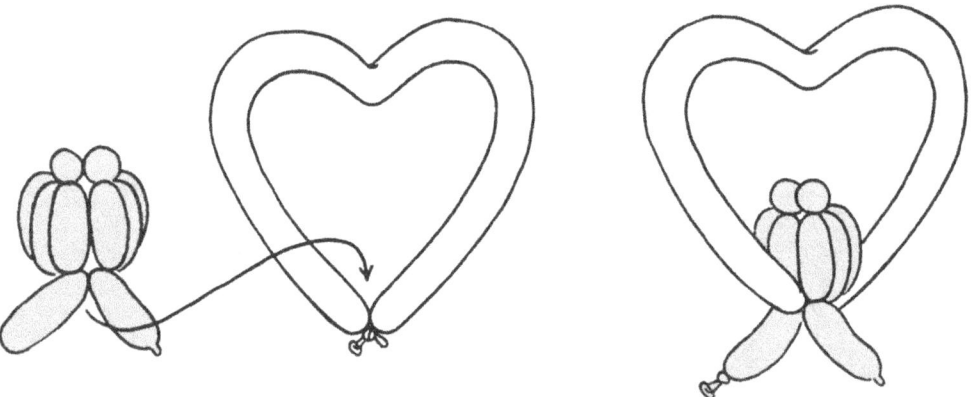

It is not always necessary to make the loop as large as possible. Smaller loops can be made and turned into heart shapes by using the squeezing technique.

HEART WAND

Inflate a 260, leaving about one inch of tail. Tie the knot.

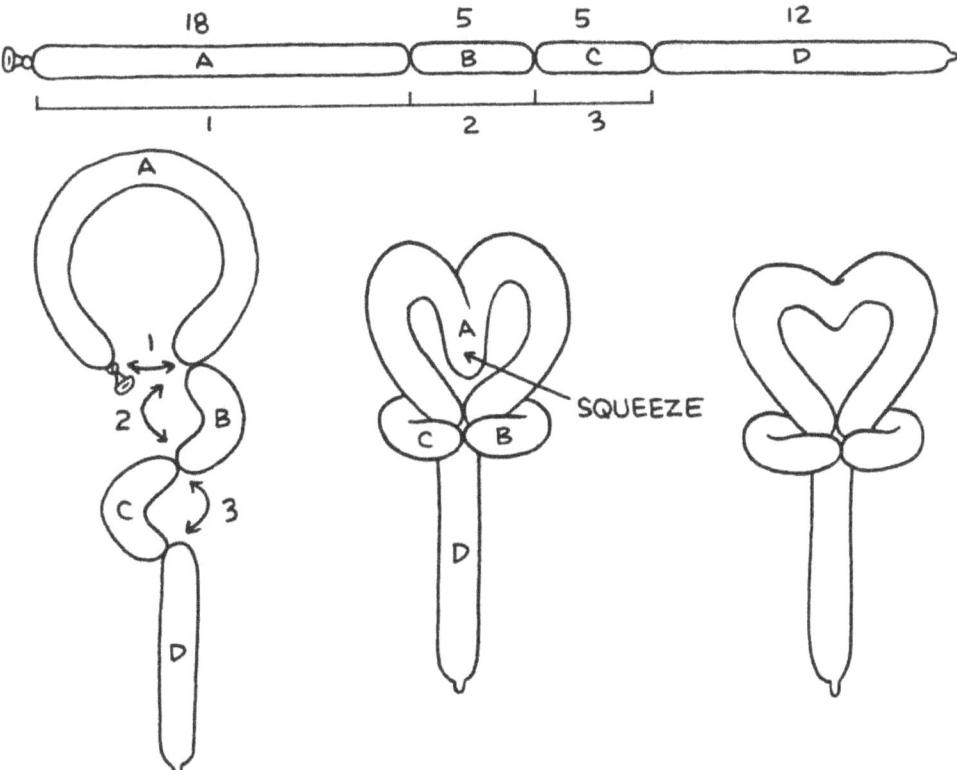

The heart shape that you have made should be large enough for you to insert an inflated six-inch heart as shown. Add a Teddy Bear and you have an irresistible balloon design!

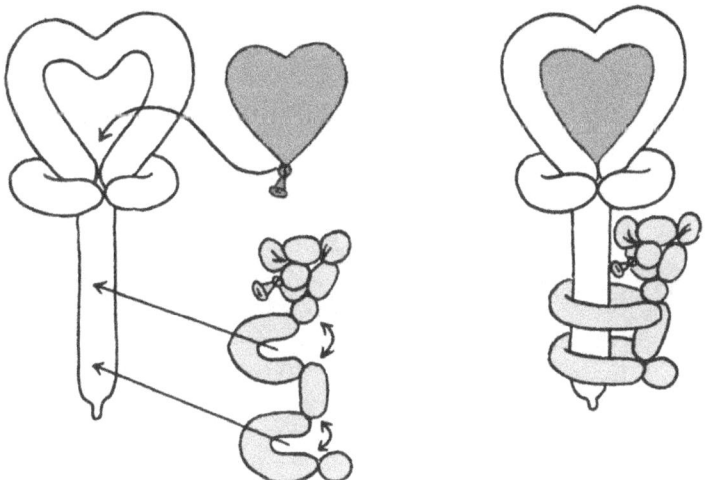

Using the smaller loops to create heart shapes also gives you the ability to make a cute little Butterfly design.

BUTTERFLY

Inflate a 260 all the way. Tie the knot. Begin as you would to make a Bee or Hummingbird. Squeeze the loops that form the wings into heart shapes, creating butterfly wings. Add another fully inflated 260 and you can "fly" your friendly Butterfly.

Beautiful flowers can be made using the six-inch heart. They make large, impressive designs that you can turn into huge bouquets of flowers simply by multiplying your creations.

HEART FLOWER

Begin with four heart balloons. Inflate them fully and tie them in pairs at their bases.

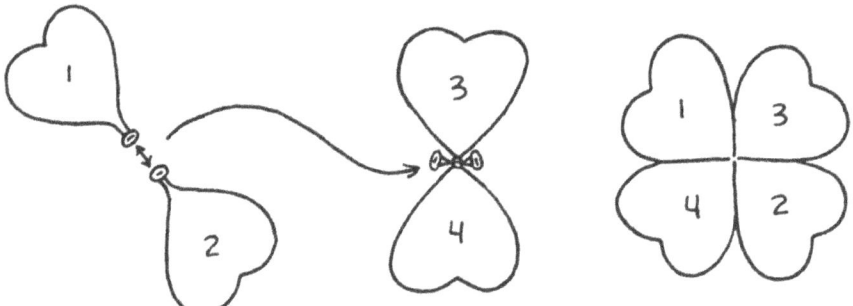

Inflate a 260, leaving about two inches of tail. Tie the knot. Begin with a tulip twist and complete as shown, adding the heart assembly as shown to create petals.

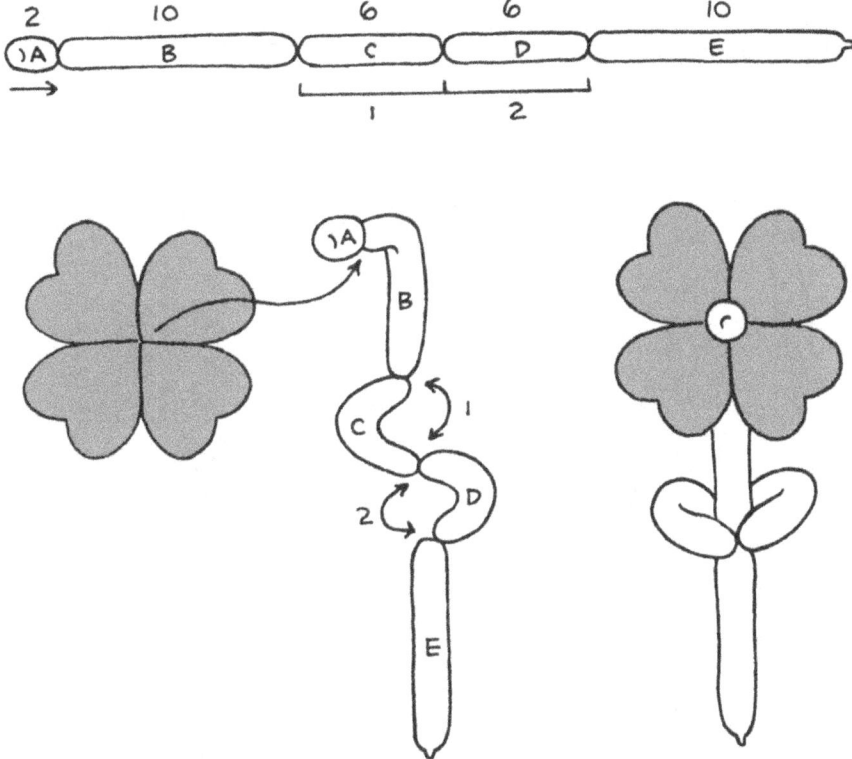

Another flower design that uses a six-inch heart balloon resembles a rosebud blooming.

ROSEBUD

Inflate a 260, leaving no tail but giving it a good burp. Tie the knot. Assemble the stem as shown. Then add the heart on top.

Be creative with your use of the heart shape and you will be impressed by the number of designs that you can make or enhance with it. The following are brief samples of some popular designs that are used by balloon artists.

Chapter Twelve

Multiple-Balloon Designs

The saying goes, "The more the merrier!" That is true with balloon designs. You have already begun to see just how much fun you can have by adding balloons to your basic hats and heart designs. Multiple-balloon designs are bigger, more colorful, and more impressive than single-balloon designs.

The multiple-balloon designs that we have covered so far in the hat and heart sections have mostly been designs where balloons were simply added or designs were combined. In this section, additional balloons will be used to create more detail. Color choices will have an important role in the designs by helping make them more identifiable. Also, there will be designs that require only portions of balloons to be used. The unused portions will be removed and discarded.

The removal of the unused portion can be a bit tricky, especially since you will be removing it after the balloon has been inflated and sculpted. The important thing is to separate the unwanted portion without damaging your work while leaving enough balloon to tie a knot.

Adding a safety bubble will enable you to do this by acting as a buffer zone between your design and the portion of the balloon to be removed. When you are ready to remove a portion of the balloon, simply make an extra bubble about two to three inches long. Grasp the balloon just above this last bubble and squeeze tightly so no air will escape when the rest of the balloon is removed. Tear or cut the remaining balloon with your nails, scissors, or some type of blade. Remember never to use your teeth to bite the balloon: Thrown bits of balloon could lodge in your throat and cause you to choke!

Now that the unwanted portion of the balloon is removed, continue to hold the remaining balloon at the point just above the safety bubble. With your other hand, squeeze the base of the safety bubble. Release the air from the top of the safety bubble and use the deflated bubble to tie a knot that will prevent any more air from escaping your design.

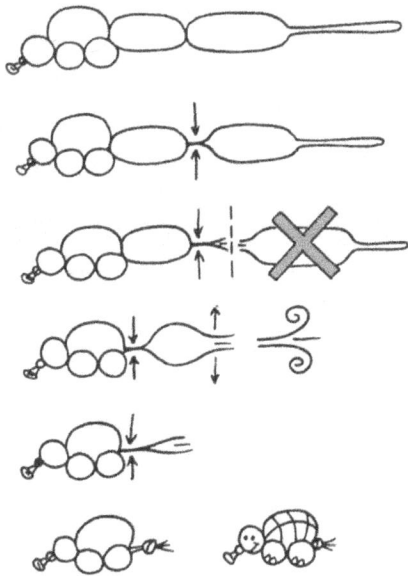

One of my favorite multiple designs that makes great use of partial balloons is the Penguin. It is a simple design that relies heavily on color selection for impact and identification and is a great exercise for the safety bubble technique.

PENGUIN

The Penguin requires three 260s: black, white, and orange.

BALLOON 1

Begin with the black 260. Inflate it, leaving about four inches of tail. Tie the knot and assemble as shown. Pull the tail of the black balloon down and squeeze it to form the neck and position the beak of the Penguin. (You will notice that this first part resembles a nearly completed Swan.)

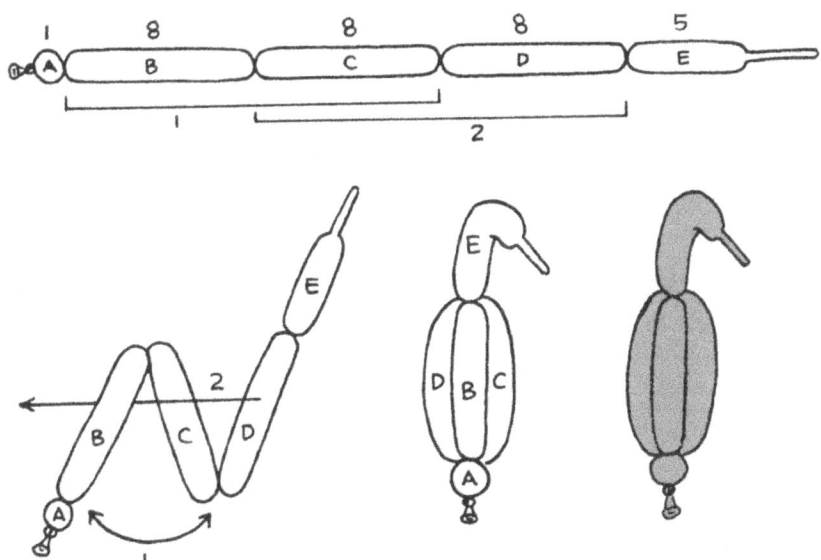

BALLOON 2

Inflate the white balloon about halfway and tie the knot. Make a fold twist around the base of the last bubble as shown, using the knot to lock the twist in place. Tuck the knot back through the completed fold twist to secure. Continue as shown and remove the excess balloon by using the safety bubble technique.

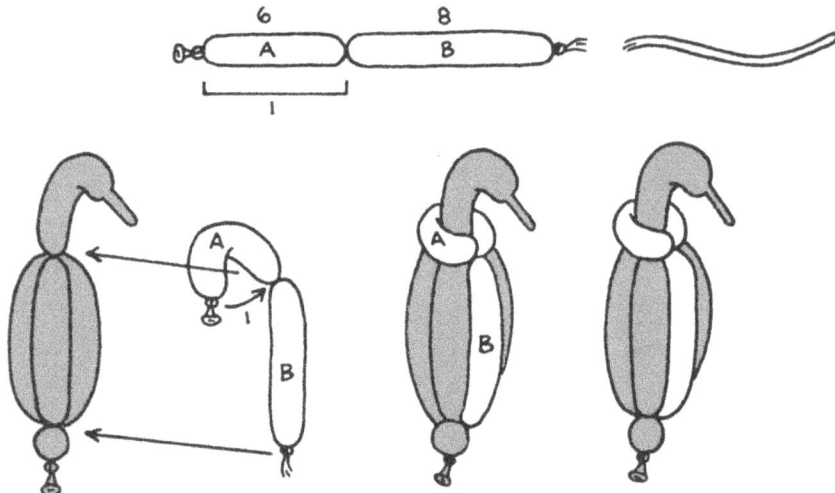

Here is an enlarged view of how to use the knot to lock a fold twist in place.

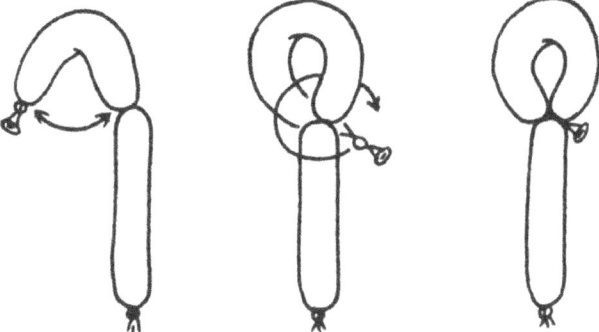

You have now completed the body of the Penguin. The orange balloon is used to make the Penguin's feet.

BALLOON 3

Inflate the orange 260 so that it is about fifteen inches long. Tie the knot. Make two fold twists as shown, one using the knot as we have just covered and the other using a standard fold twist. Remove the excess balloon by using the safety bubble and attach the completed feet as shown.

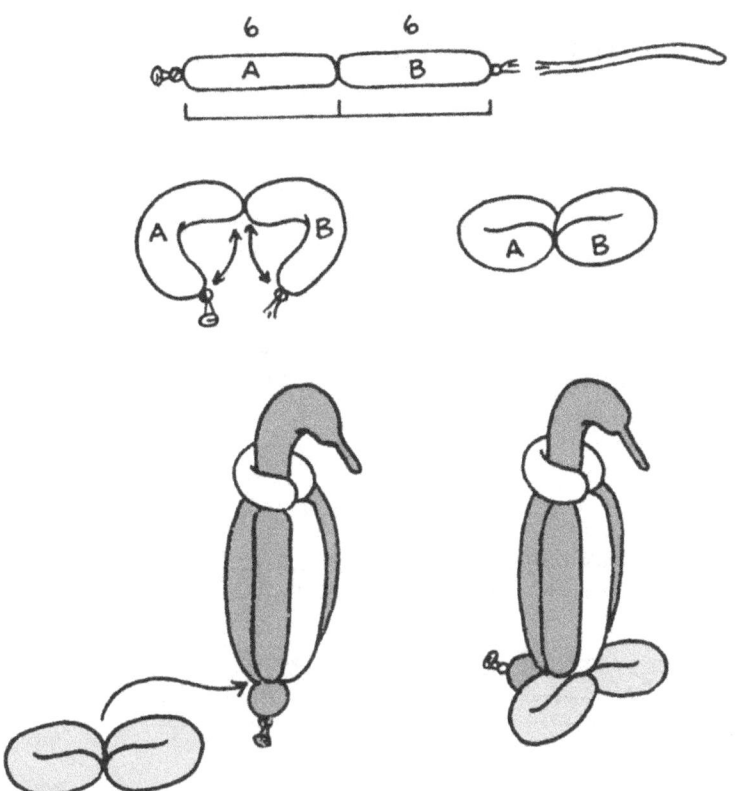

This perky Penguin stands on his own and is quite an eye-catcher!

LOBSTER

The contrasting colors that were used to create the Penguin made it interesting to look at and helped to define what it was. Some designs, however, require that the same color balloons be used throughout, as is the case with this Lobster design. It uses two red 260s to make its body and claws, which would look strange if they were different colors.

BALLOON 1

Inflate the first red 260, leaving about five or six inches of tail. Tie the knot. Begin with a split twist, using the knot to lock the twist in place.

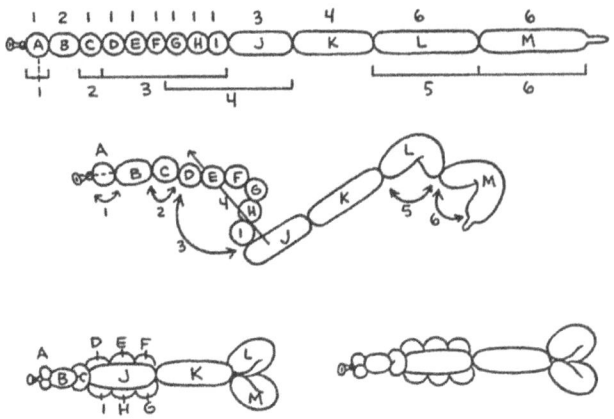

BALLOON 2

Inflate the second red 260, leaving about six inches of tail. Tie the knot. Note that you will not be using the whole balloon and will need to use a safety bubble to remove the unwanted portion.

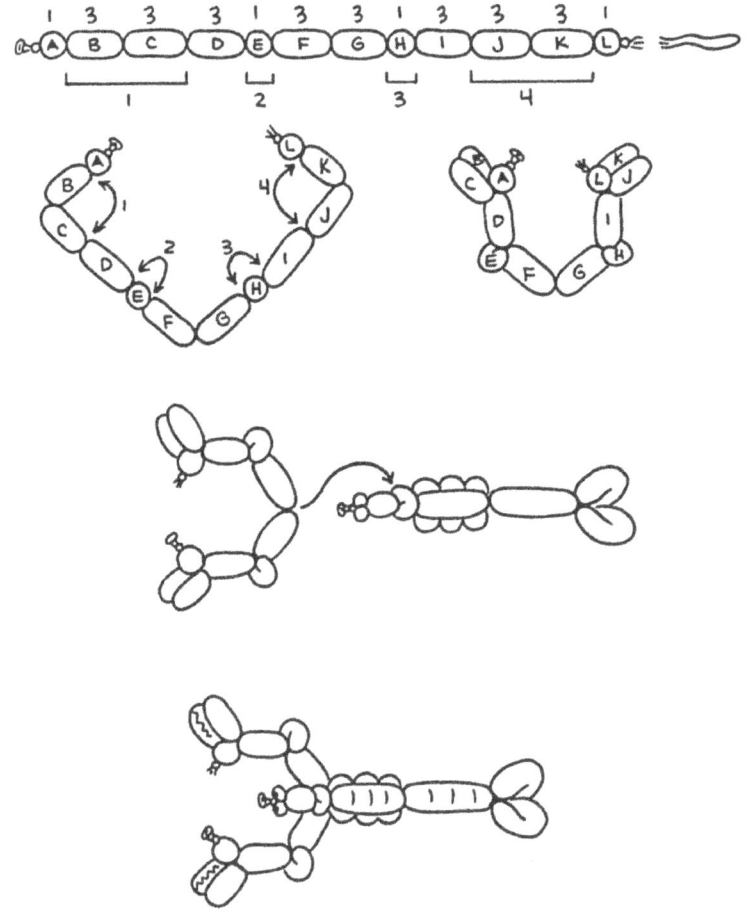

MERMAID

The Lobster has an underwater friend that is one of my favorite multiple-balloon designs, the

Mermaid. The Mermaid is made with three 260s. Color, again, plays a big part in defining the design. Green is used for her tail and fins. Pink is used for her torso. The color you choose for her hair is optional. Yellow, red, orange, black, or brown can all be good colors to use.

BALLOON 1

The first balloon is used to make her hair. Choose the color you wish to use and inflate it, leaving about three inches of tail. Tie the knot.

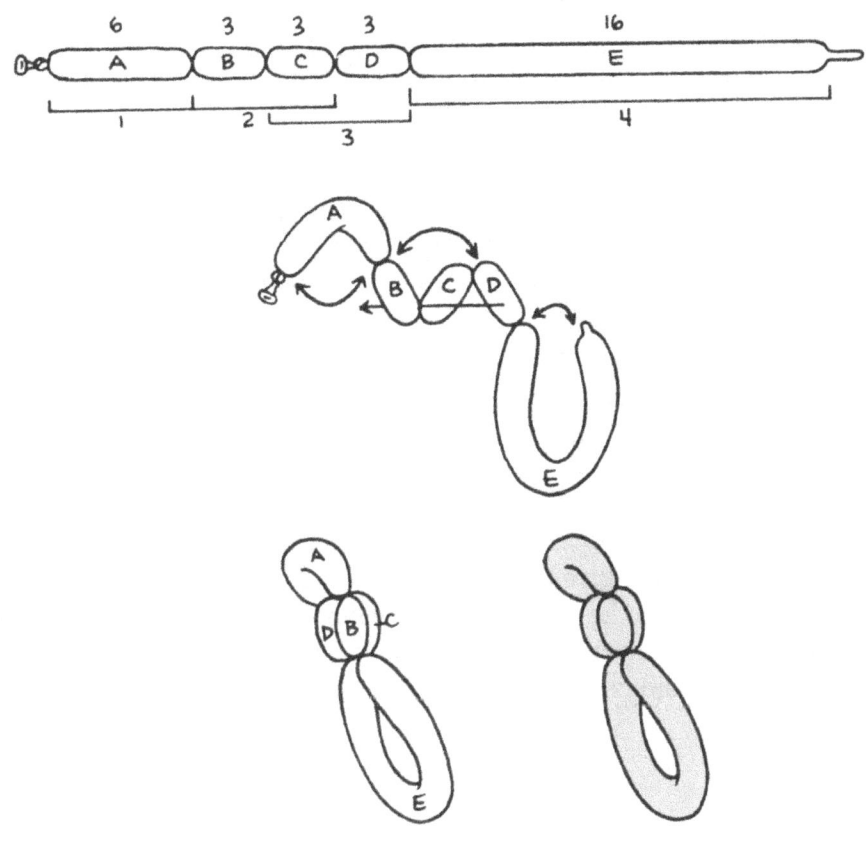

BALLOON 2

Inflate the pink balloon about three-quarters full. You will not be using the whole balloon, so plan to use the safety bubble to remove any excess. Once you have inflated the balloon and tied the knot, attach the knotted end to balloon 1 as shown. Make the first bubble that is shown on the diagram and lock that in place on balloon 1 as shown.

Continue following the diagram, noting the pop twist that is used to create the arms. It is best to pop this bubble after the entire design is complete.

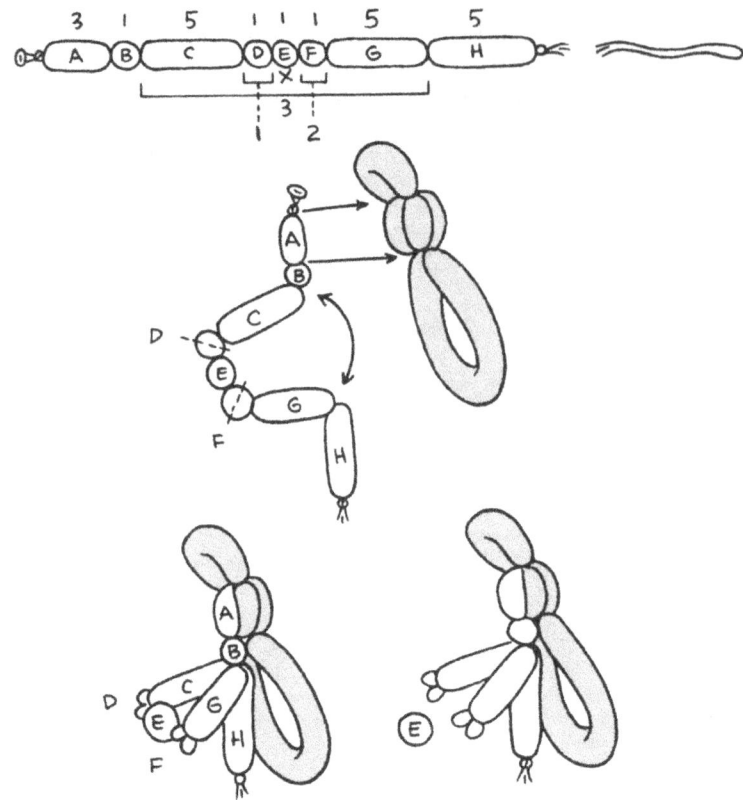

BALLOON 3

Inflate the green balloon fully and give it a good burp. Tie the knot. You will notice that the tail of the Mermaid is very similar to the stem of the Rosebud, ending with two longer bubbles to create the fins. Once balloon 3 is completed, attach it to the body of the Mermaid. Pop the pop twist and your friendly Mermaid is complete!

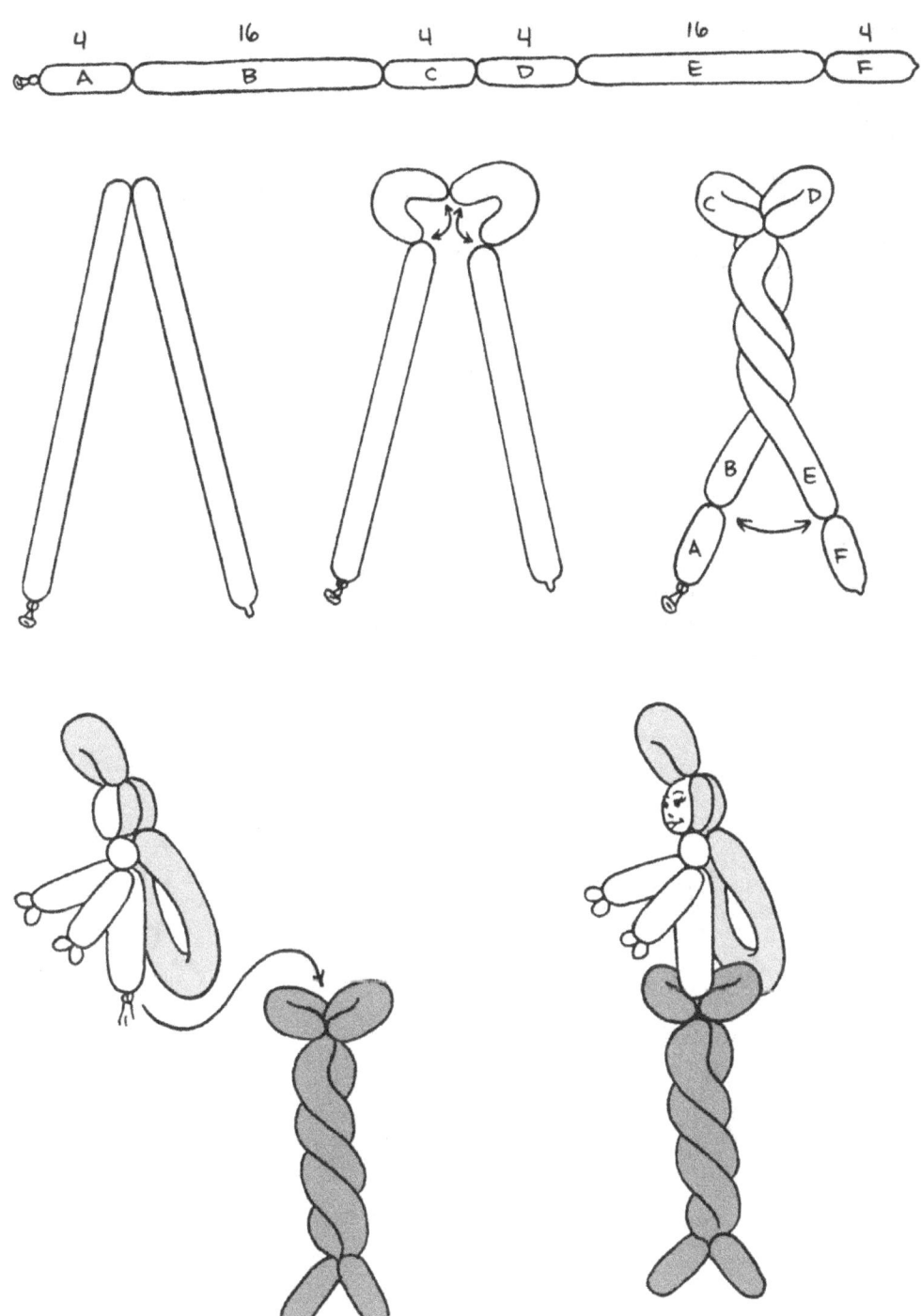

If only the Mermaid had legs, she'd be able to ride this next design! The Bicycle is an impressive balloon design and is well worth practicing. Once you get the hang of it, I'm sure you will want to make figures to ride it.

BICYCLE

The Bicycle is made with five 260s. Color is not so important, but you may want to make wheels one color and the frame another.

BALLOON 1

Inflate the balloon fully and give it a good burp. Tie the knot. This will be the handlebars.

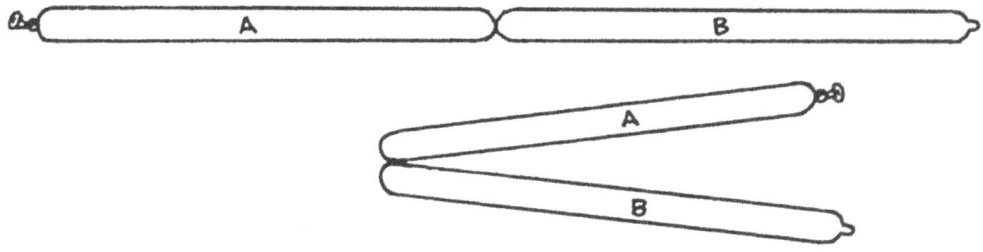

BALLOON 2

Inflate this balloon fully and tie the knot. Attach it to balloon 1 and coil it around itself as shown, making a wheel shape. Lock the coil, using the two sides of balloon 1 as shown. This forms the front wheel and handlebars.

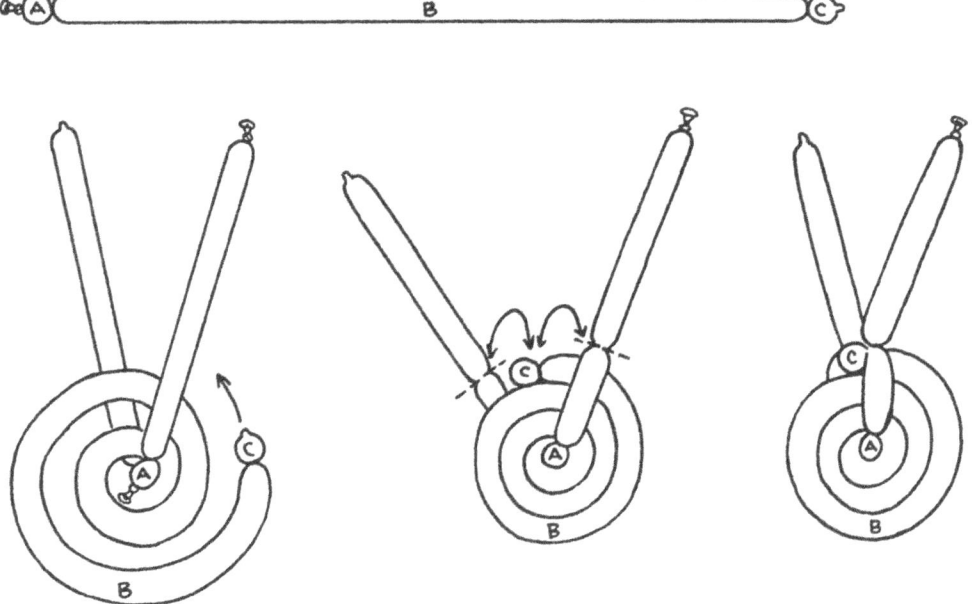

BALLOONS 3 AND 4

Inflate both balloons fully and give them both a good burp. Tie their knots and attach to each other as shown. These will be the bike's frame and back fork.

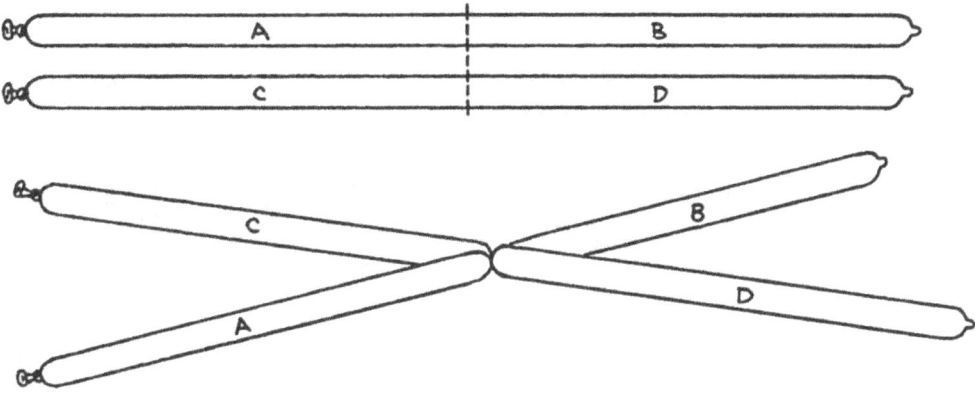

BALLOON 5

Inflate this balloon fully and tie the knot. Create the back wheel in the same manner as the front wheel by making a coil. Lock it in place by using balloons 3 and 4 as shown.

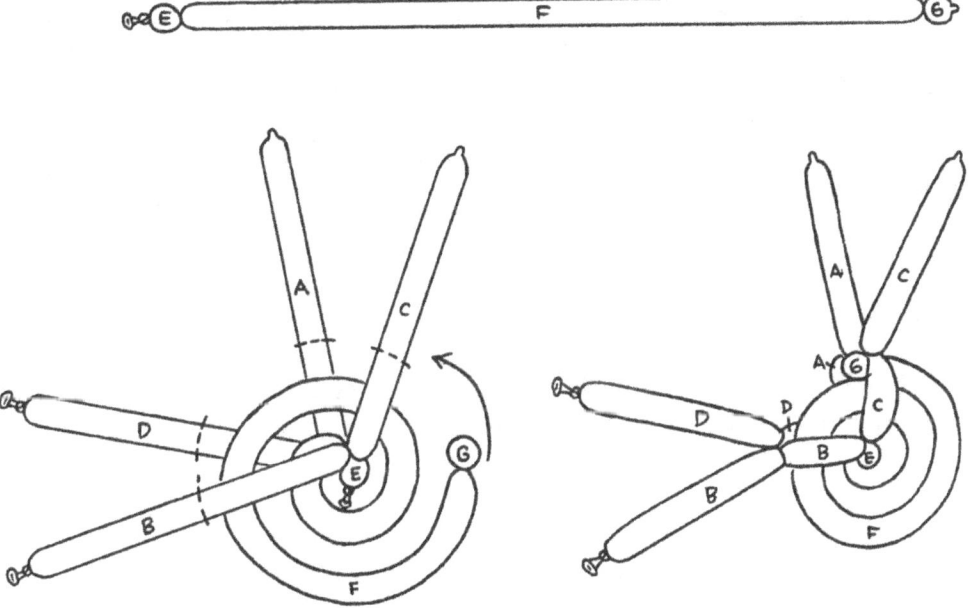

Now that you have assembled the front and back wheels of the bicycle, attach the two sections together. The frame of the bike will become complete and the seat will be formed. Finally, bend the handlebars as noted for the best effect. You are ready to roll!

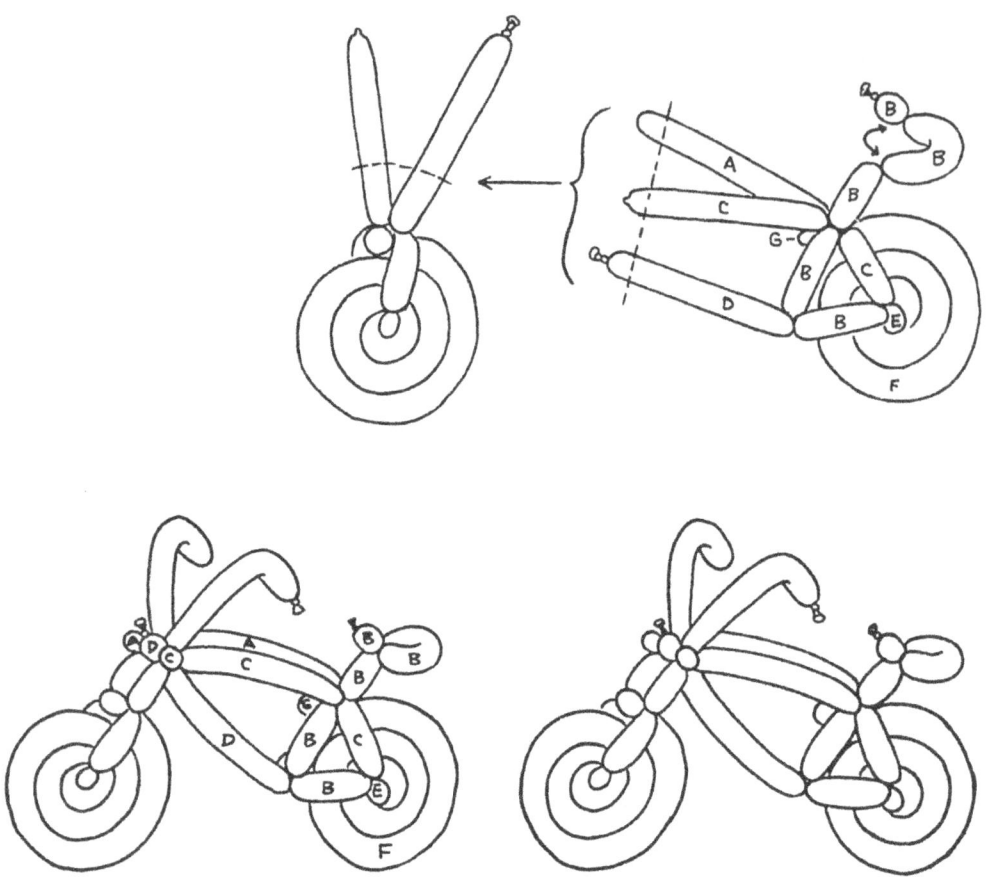

OCTOPUS

A very fun and large design that is simple to make is the Octopus. It requires five balloons: four 260s and one large round balloon. Inflate all five balloons fully and attach as shown.

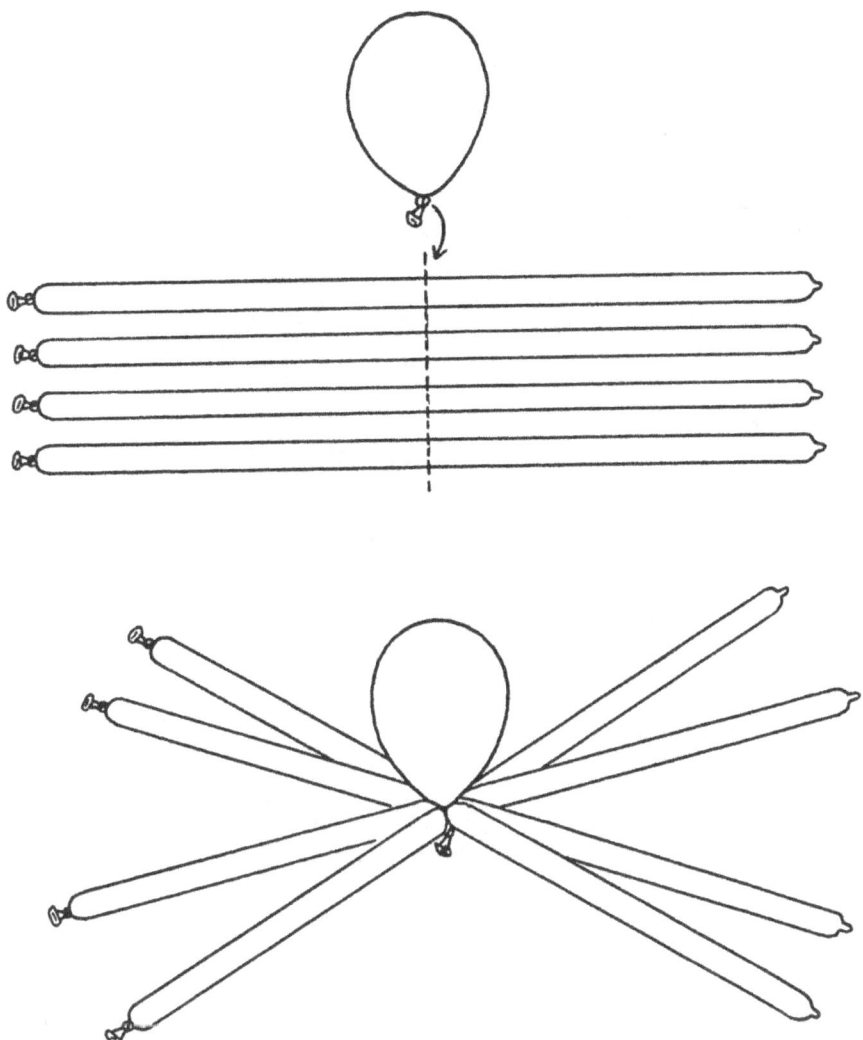

Twist the legs of the Octopus around your hand one at a time to give extra character, and your design will come to life!

This design is particularly impressive when the round balloon is filled with helium and the Octopus floats in the air! The larger the round balloon, the more floating power your design will have.

(Because of their shape and size, 260s do not respond well to the powers of helium. Fully inflated with helium, a 260 will contain just enough helium to lift its weight. If you need to allow for any tail at all to make your design, it probably will not float.)

SPIDER

The Octopus has a buddy who also sports eight legs. The Spider can be made with five 260s. Black is usually a good color for big ugly spiders, but I must admit that the Spider looks great in any color!

BALLOON 1

Inflate the first 260, leaving about three inches of tail. Tie the knot and make the Spider's body as shown, using two roll-throughs.

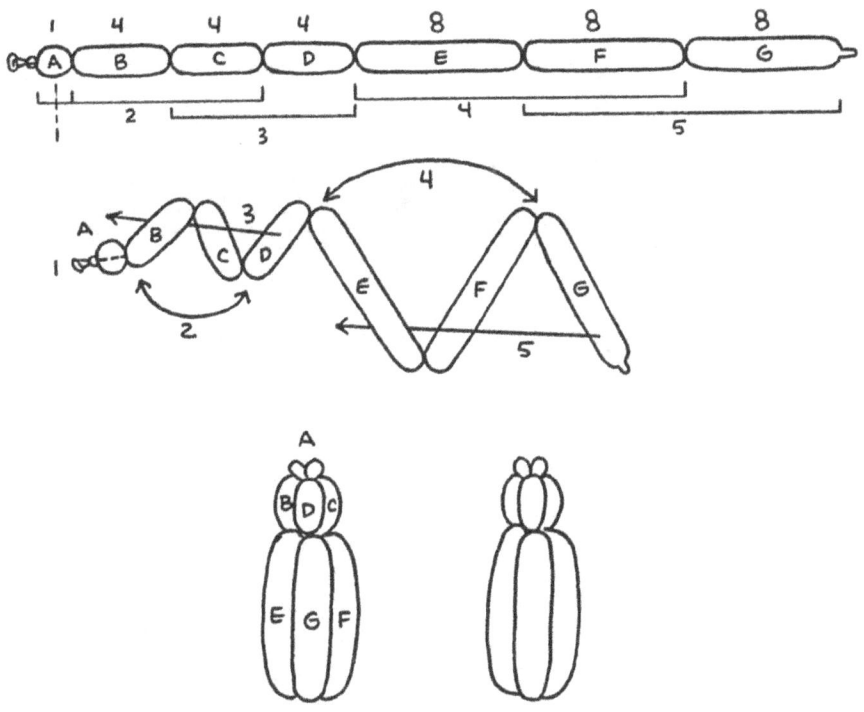

BALLOONS 2–8

Inflate the remaining balloons fully and give them all a good burp. Tie their knots and join them at the center as you did with the Octopus design.

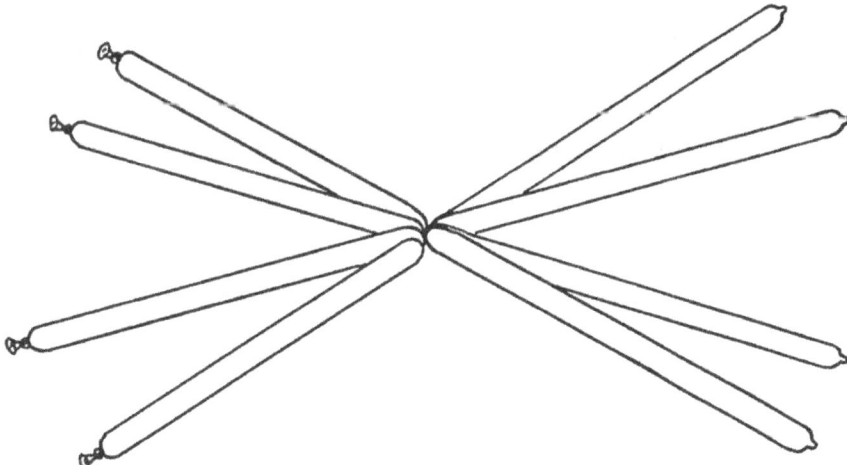

Slide the legs through the larger roll-through of the Spider's body so that the center of the legs sits inside the three bubbles that form the roll-through. Two bubbles should sit on top and one on the bottom. Fan the legs out as shown.

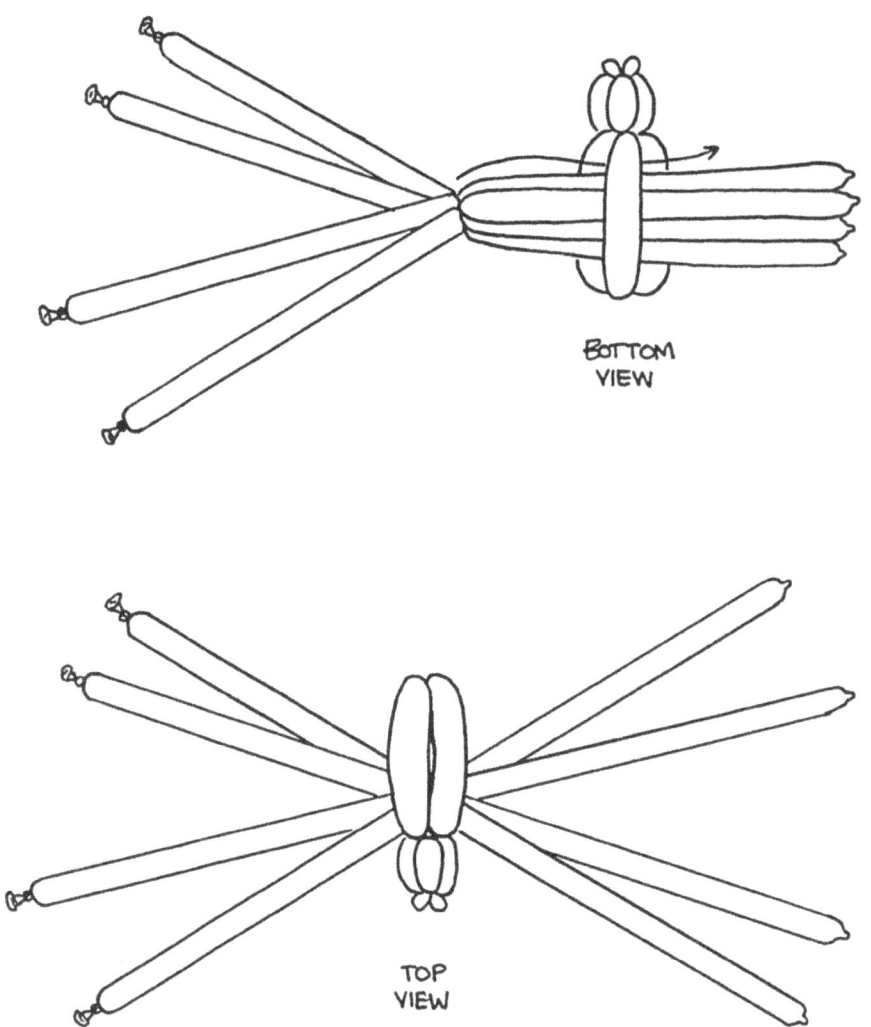

Find the center of each leg. Bend the leg in half and make a small fold twist for a joint or a knee on each leg.

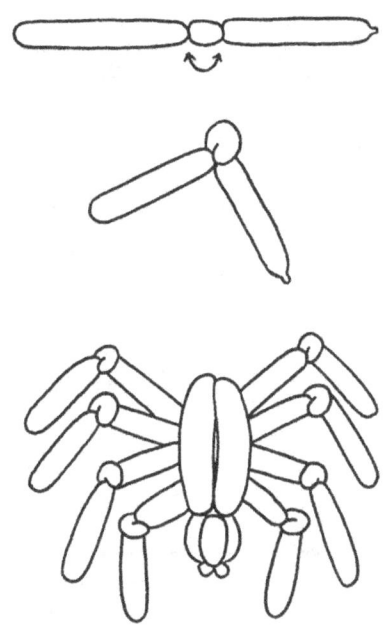

LITTLE RED WAGON

The Spider design reminds us how the fold twist or the ear twist can change the direction of the 260 by forming a corner or a joint. This element will become very useful in constructing a box shape that we will use to make a Little Red Wagon.

This design requires a lot of 260s—seventeen to be exact! Don't let this discourage you, because most of the balloons are used to make the wheels and are only partially used. As you develop your skills you will discover that you can economize by reusing portions of balloons that are removed.

The colors in this design are important for the final effect. You will need eight red balloons, five black balloons, and four white balloons.

Begin with four red balloons. Inflate them, leaving about three inches of tail on each. Tie their knots. Form the box of the wagon as shown.

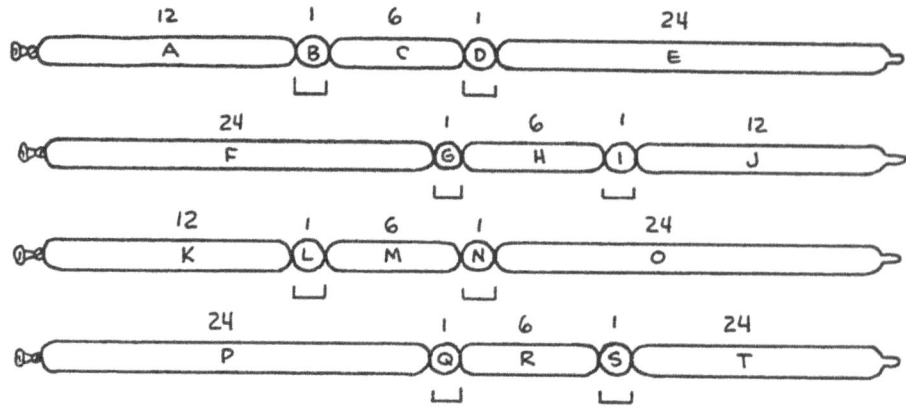

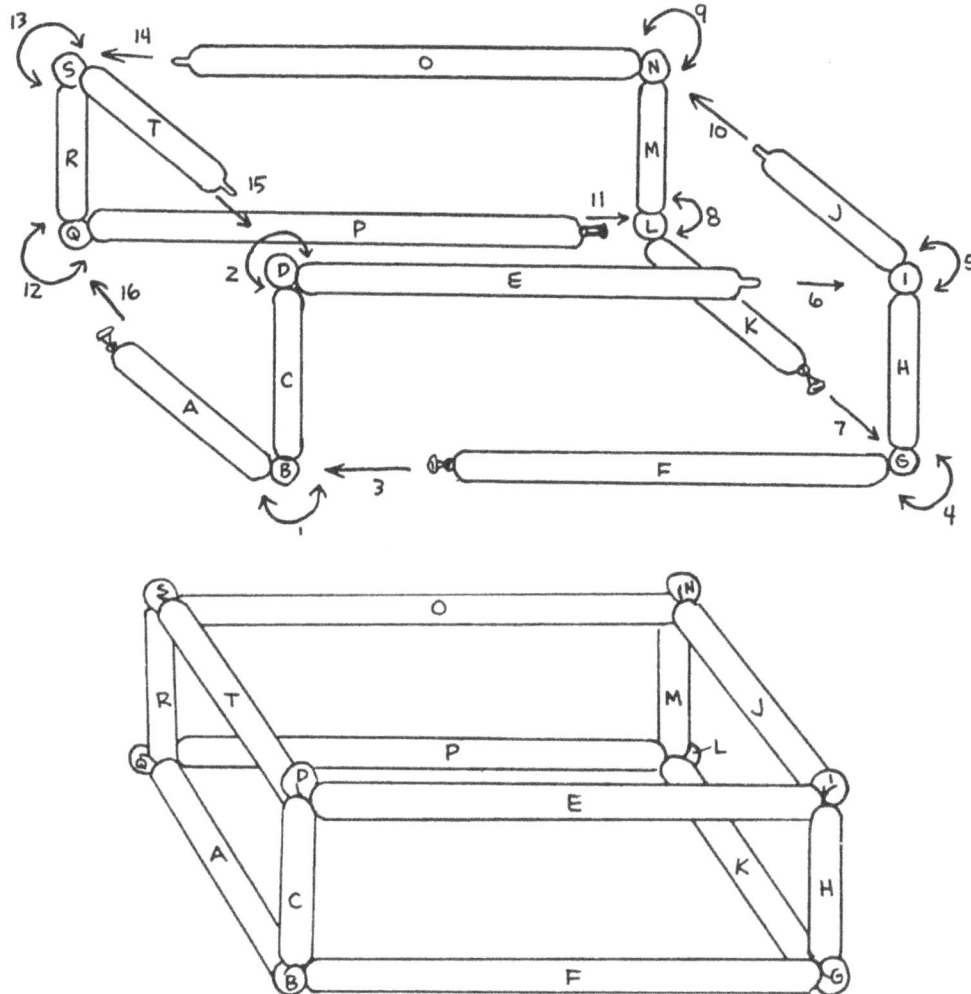

Complete the box and set it aside. Now take one black, one white, and one red balloon. Inflate the black 260 so that it is more than a foot long. Tie the knot. Make a loop as shown and remove the excess balloon.

Inflate the white balloon so that it is about eight inches long. Make a smaller loop, discarding the excess balloon. Fit the white loop inside the black loop as shown.

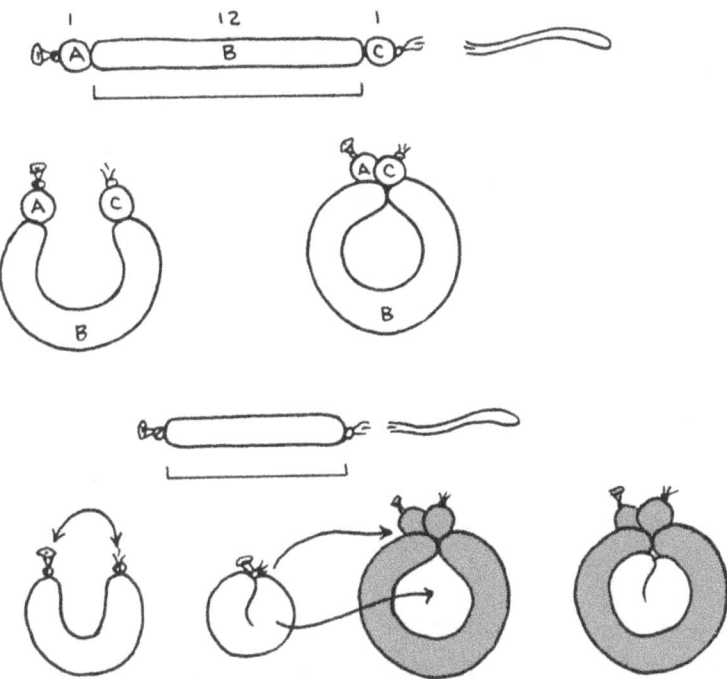

Finally, cut about three inches off the tip of the red balloon. Inflate the tip to form a round bubble and tie a knot at the base of the bubble. Tie another knot about a half an inch away from the first knot and insert the balloon into the center of the wheel as shown.

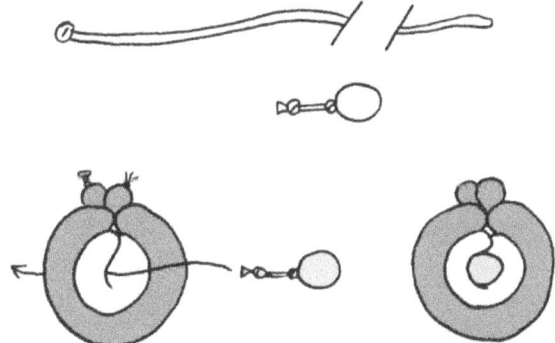

Make four of these wheels. Try to get them all to be the same size! Once they are complete, attach them to the box as shown.

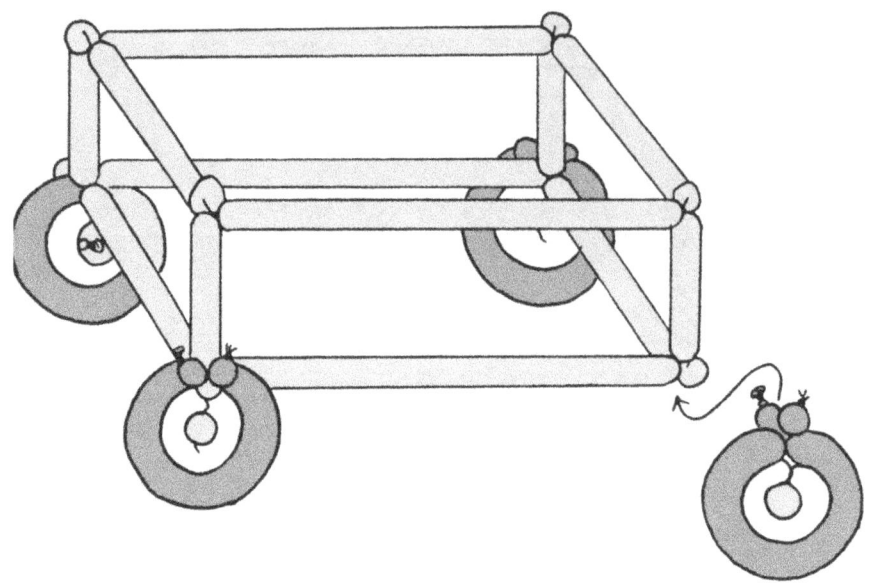

The last balloon will make the handle and floor of the wagon. Inflate a black 260, leaving about three inches of tail. Tie the knot. Turn the wagon over and attach as shown.

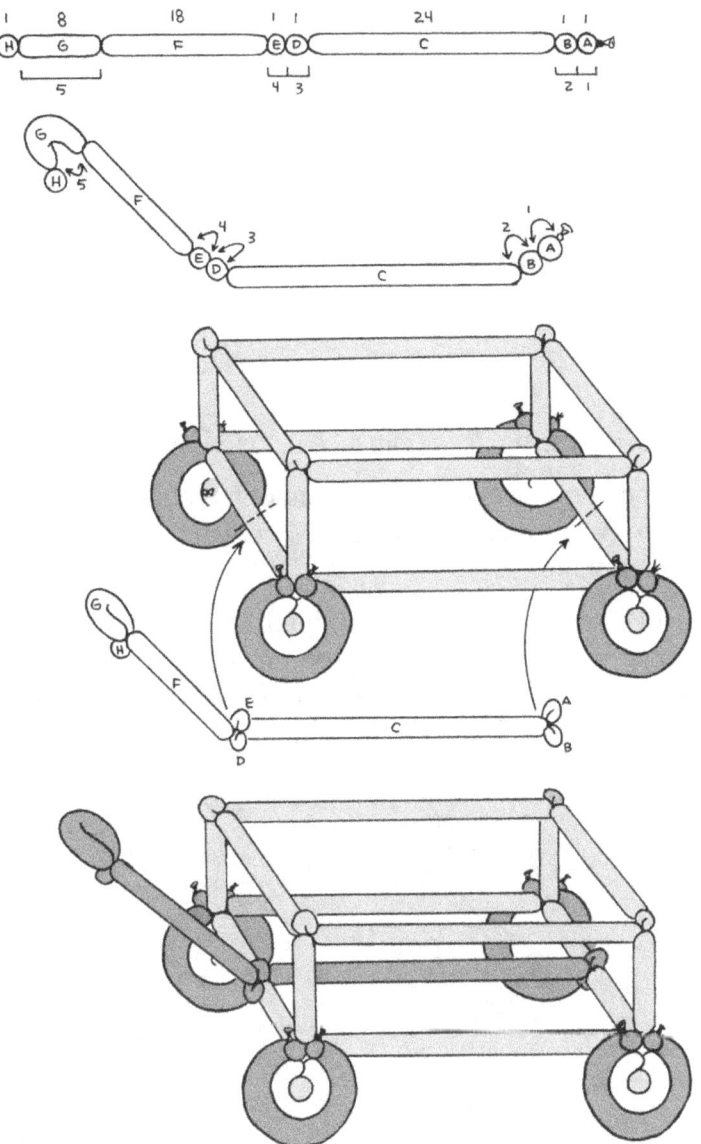

The end result is a beautiful Little Red Wagon that you can fill with heart balloons, animal designs, or flowers, or just let it speak for itself!

Chapter Thirteen

Balloon Cartoons

Cartooning has always been a passion of mine. I began my career as a clown doing caricatures for children and drawing cartoons on helium balloons. I had successfully tapped into my experience as a professional cartoonist to enhance my clowning abilities.

A few years later I learned how to make animals out of balloons. I think I was attracted to this new skill for the same reasons I liked cartooning. My creations were simplified or exaggerated likenesses of the intended subjects.

Since then I have discovered that there is a more fundamental similarity between the two mediums. As a student of cartooning, I had learned to build images of figures out of basic shapes, primarily spheres and cylinders. Looking at my balloon creations, I realized that those same shapes correspond to the bubbles used in balloon designs.

Having come to this realization, I began to create cartoonlike characters out of balloons. These multiple-balloon designs were big, fun, and goofy looking. My cartoon balloons became instantly popular and were recognized with awards at major clown conventions.

More importantly, other balloon artists around the country have begun to see new possibilities in balloon art through cartoons, and a whole new wave of balloon sculpting is emerging.

This chapter will focus on some basic cartoon designs. You will notice that by making color choices and adding details, it is possible to transform these basics into many of your favorite cartoon characters. I encourage you to build on these designs and depart from them, using them as a springboard for your own artistry!

Most of the following designs, like most cartoon characters, are animals with human characteristics. They have heads, bodies, arms, and legs, with animal features like ears, tails, and beaks attached.

Building the heads and bodies of some of these designs requires building some volume into their shapes so that they will appear proportionate to the arms and legs of the figure. To do this, the roll-through is used to create fuller shapes like the ones shown below.

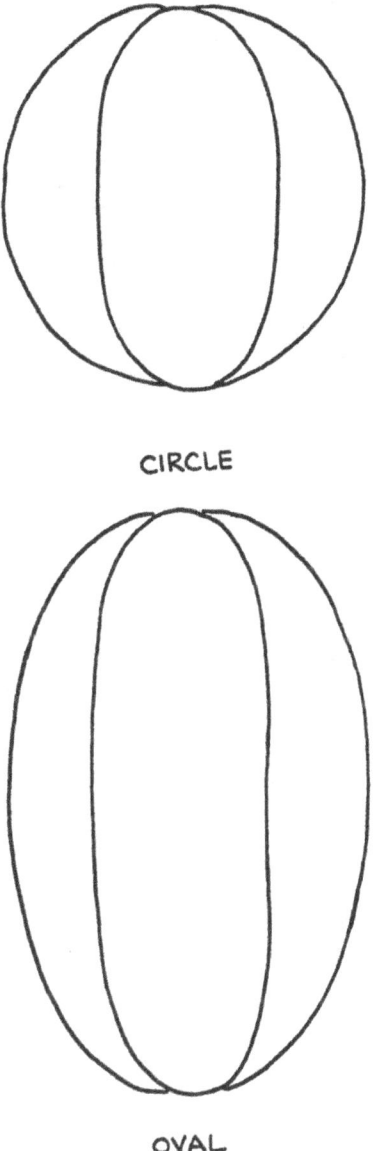

CIRCLE

OVAL

We will begin with a figure that you already have some familiarity with: the Teddy Bear. We will, however, make him much bigger, more cartoony, and more huggable!

BIG OL' BEAR

This Big Ol' Bear requires three 260s. I recommend that they all be the same color.

BALLOON 1

Inflate the balloon, leaving about three to four inches of tail. Tie the knot and make the head and body as shown.

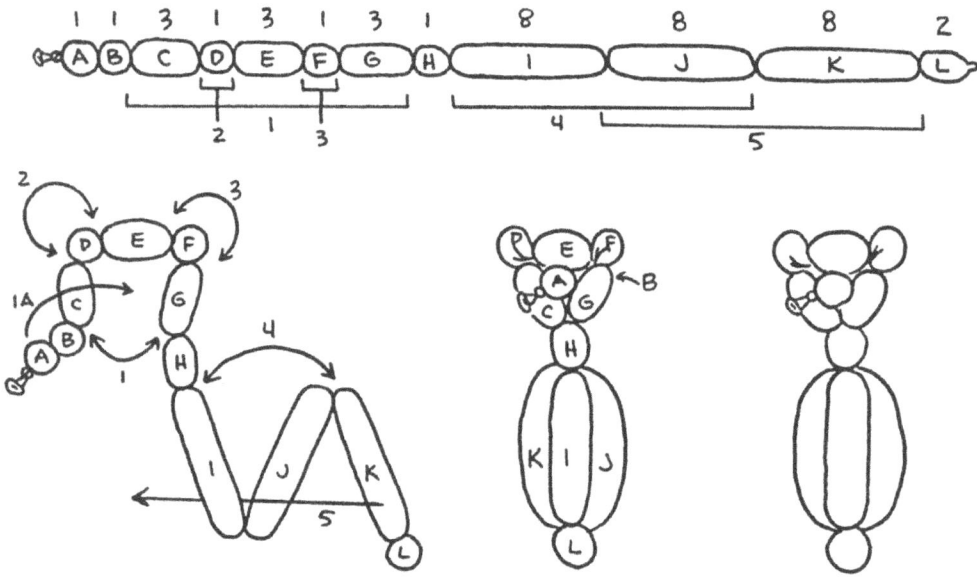

BALLOON 2

Inflate the balloon, leaving about one inch of tail. Tie the knot and complete the arms as shown. Make both hands first, then fold the arms in half and make a small fold twist at the center.

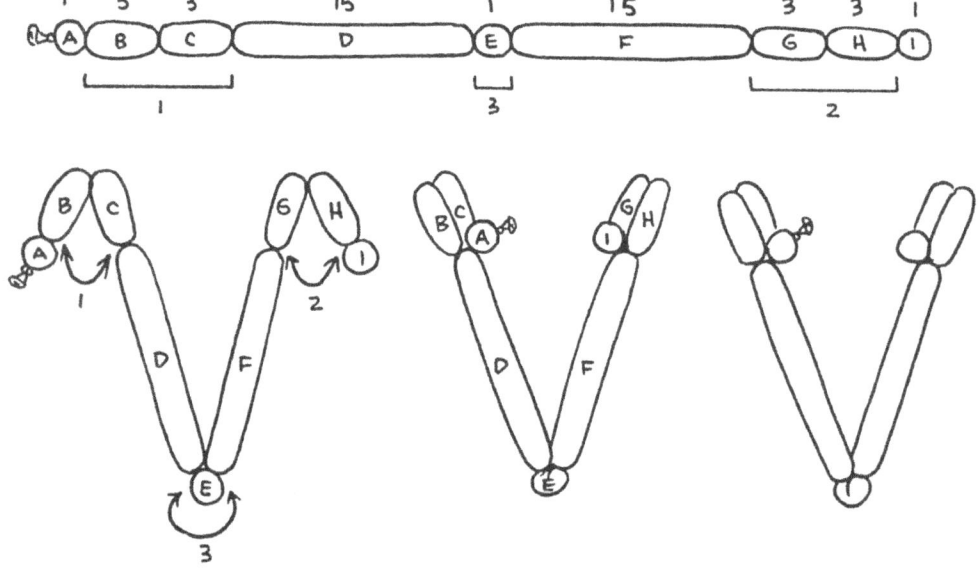

BALLOON 3

Inflate the balloon, leaving about one inch of tail. Tie the knot and complete the legs as shown. Notice that the feet, though similar to the hands, use larger bubbles and that there is no fold twist in the center.

Attach the arms and legs to the body of our bear friend as shown.

The fold twist on the arms helps to stabilize them at the base of the neck.

The legs are naturally stabilized by the bear's tail.

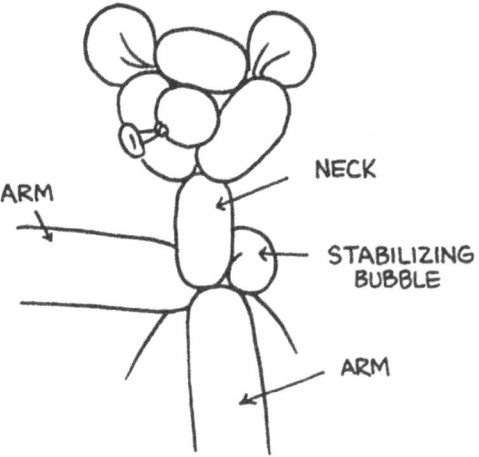

Big Ol' Bear is huggable. Just wrap him around someone and lock his hands and feet together.

BIG OL' CAT

You can make Big Ol' Bear into a Big Ol' Cat very easily by tucking his tail inside of the roll-through that forms his body. Inflate another 260 fully and attach it at the base of the body, using the knot of the new balloon. Wrap it around your hand to give it character, and your critter is now a cat with a long tail.

I hope you are starting to realize how easy it is to transform these characters from one to another!

The Bear and Cat designs that we have just gone over are built on a basic body with arms and legs. These same features are uniform for many of my designs. We will change the head on this next design and add some ears to make a Crazy Rabbit.

CRAZY RABBIT

This design requires four 260s. White is usually a good choice for bunnies!

BALLOON 1

Inflate the balloon leaving about three inches of tail. Tie the knot and make the head and body as shown.

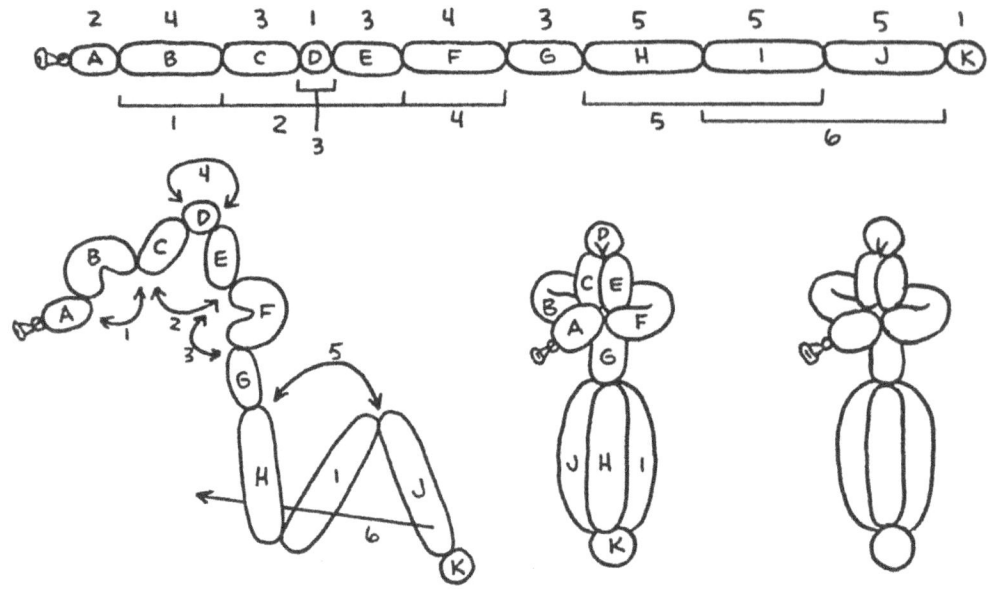

BALLOON 2

Inflate the balloon, leaving about a half an inch of tail. Make a large loop and tie both ends together. Divide the loop in half as shown and squeeze the ends to form pointy rabbit ears. Attach to the head as shown.

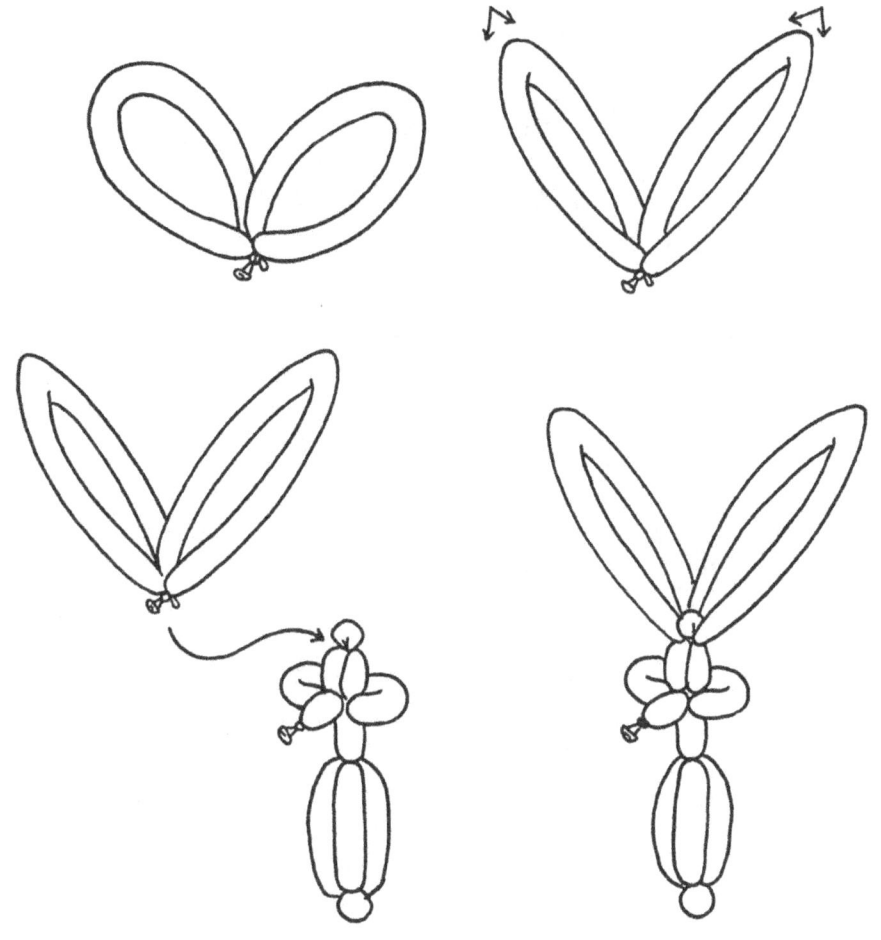

BALLOONS 3 AND 4

Make arms and legs out of balloons 3 and 4 as you did in the Bear design. Attach them to the body of the Rabbit.

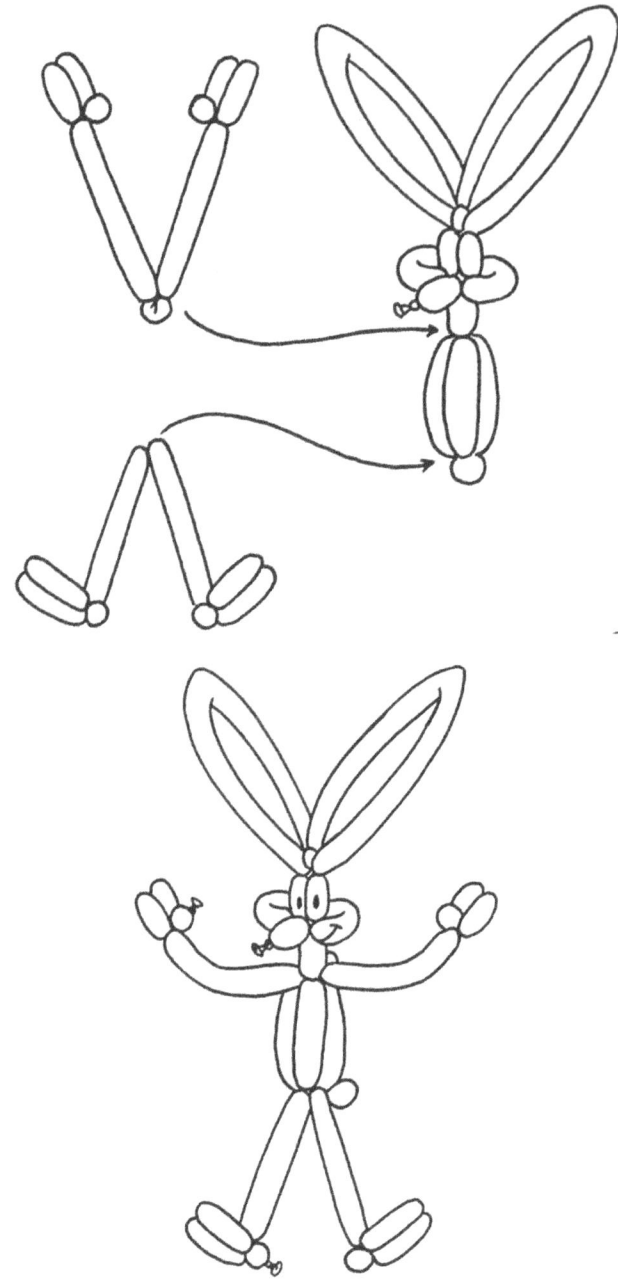

This design is a Crazy Rabbit for sure! You can make some minor changes and turn this hare into a Coyote or a Mouse as shown on the next page.

COYOTE OR WOLF

Use either black or brown balloons to make the design. Tuck the Rabbit's small tail into the body and add a slightly longer tail by partially inflating another 260 and removing the unused portion by using a safety bubble.

MOUSE

Make the Mouse by shaping the ears as circles instead of long ovals. Tuck in the Rabbit's tail and add a 260 that has only been inflated one inch. The long, skinny tail is the perfect final touch.

I have always been a big fan of cartoon ducks, so it was no surprise to me that my first true cartoon balloon design was of a duck. This design continues to be one of my favorites.

DIPPY DUCK

This design requires four 260s. Two should be orange. The other two can be any other color so long as they are both the same. For this example we will use yellow.

BALLOON 1

Inflate a yellow balloon, leaving about two to three inches of tail. Tie the knot and assemble as shown.

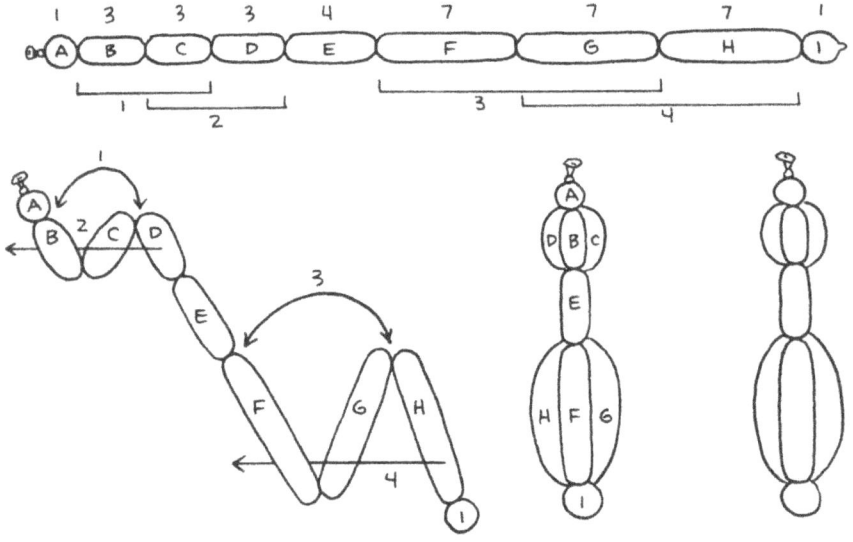

BALLOONS 2 AND 3

Make yellow arms out of balloon 2 and orange legs out of balloon 3.

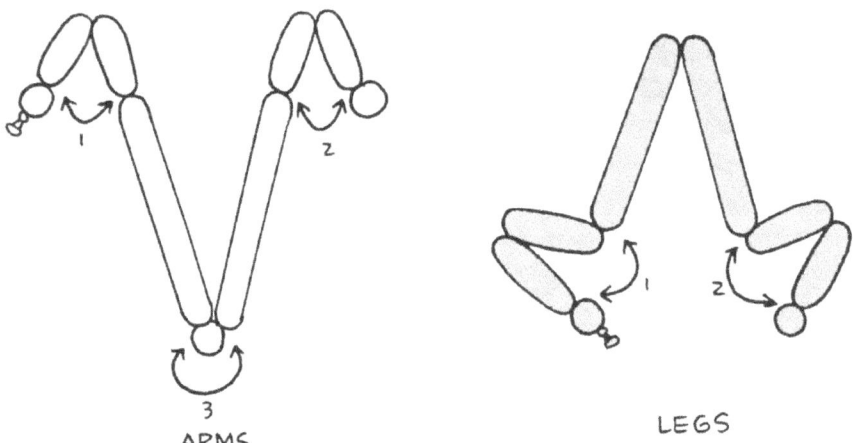

Attach the arms and legs to the body as shown.

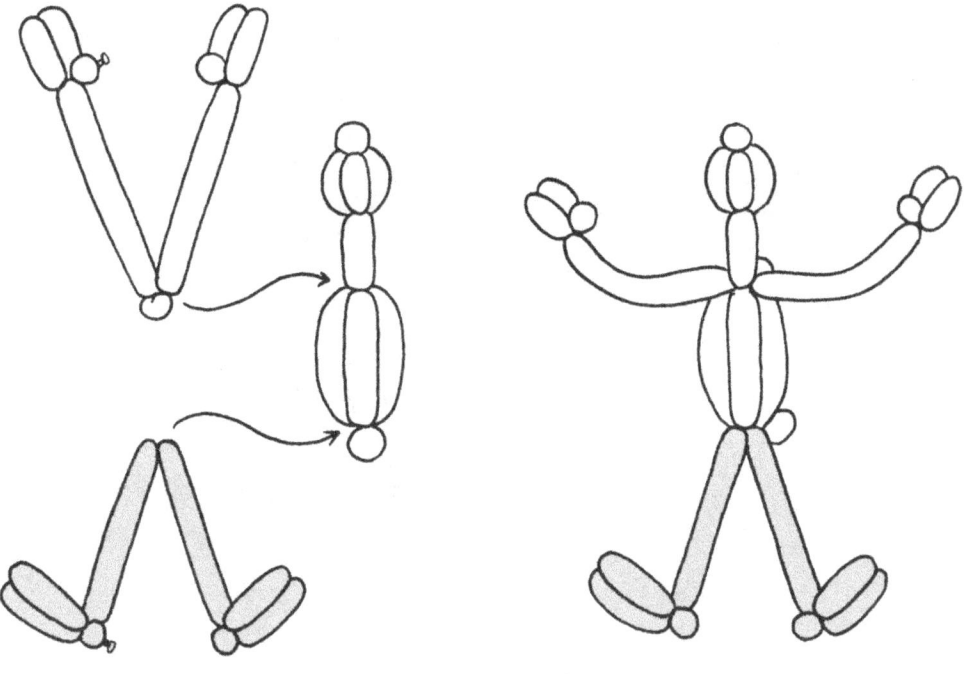

BALLOON 4

Inflate an orange balloon, leaving about six inches of tail. Tie the knot. Make the Duck's bill as shown. Remove any excess balloon by using the safety bubble technique.

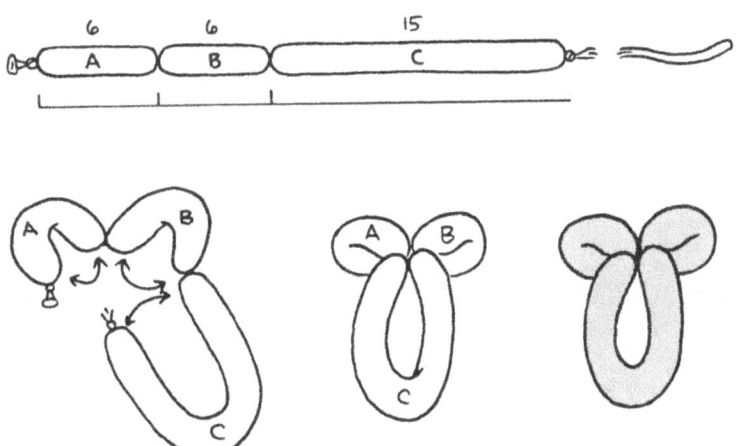

Attach the bill to the base of the head as shown and bend the front of the bill upward for that ducky look!

Try adding these different beaks, wings, and tails to transform Dippy into a host of other Bouncy Birds!

STORK

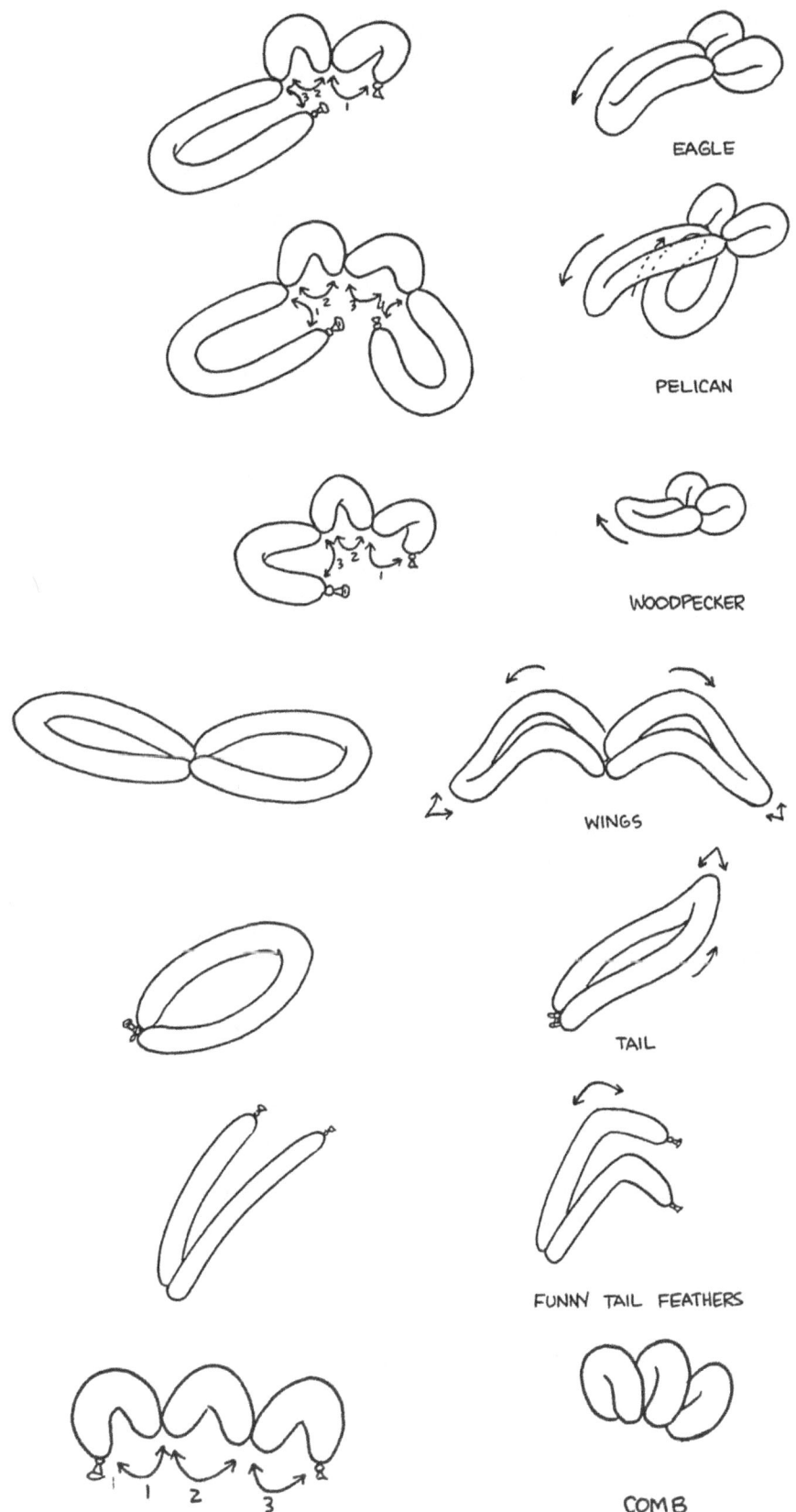

Here are some illustrations of what some of those birds might look like. Remember, you can use color to enhance the type of bird you are designing.

It is a lot of fun to add detail to cartoon designs. The additional balloons add extra color and character to the designs. Two of the most simple additions to cartoon designs are noses and eyes. They require a minimal amount of effort, and the results will bring your cartoon balloon to life.

These extras can be added to most of the cartoon designs that we have already covered, but we will use a new design to learn how to add them. Who could be a more appropriate subject than Rudolph the Red-Nosed Reindeer?!

RUDOLPH THE RED-NOSED REINDEER

To make Rudy with a red nose and white eyes will require six 260s: three brown, one black, one red, and one white.

BALLOON 1

Cut about three inches off the tip of a red balloon. Inflate it so that the tip is round. Tie a knot at the base of the bubble. There will be some balloon left over; tie a knot at the end of that. This is known as an anchor knot.

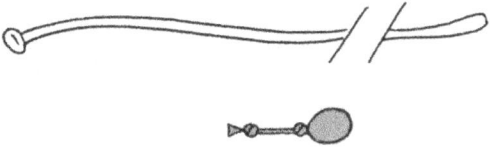

BALLOON 2

Inflate a brown balloon, leaving about four inches of tail. Tie the knot. Align the anchor knot from balloon 1 with the knot on balloon 2. Press both knots into the body of the balloon and make a tulip twist, locking both knots in place. Be sure to press both knots in far enough so that the red bubble is seated firmly in the tulip twist.

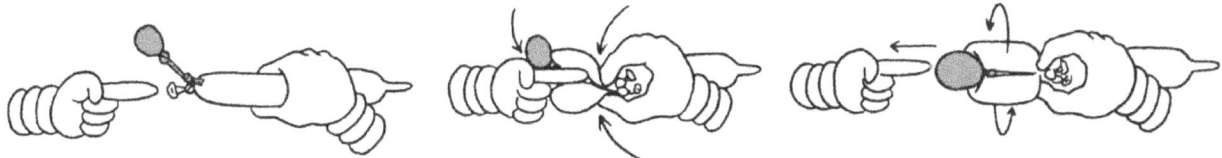

Rudolph's nose is now in place. Complete the head and body as shown.

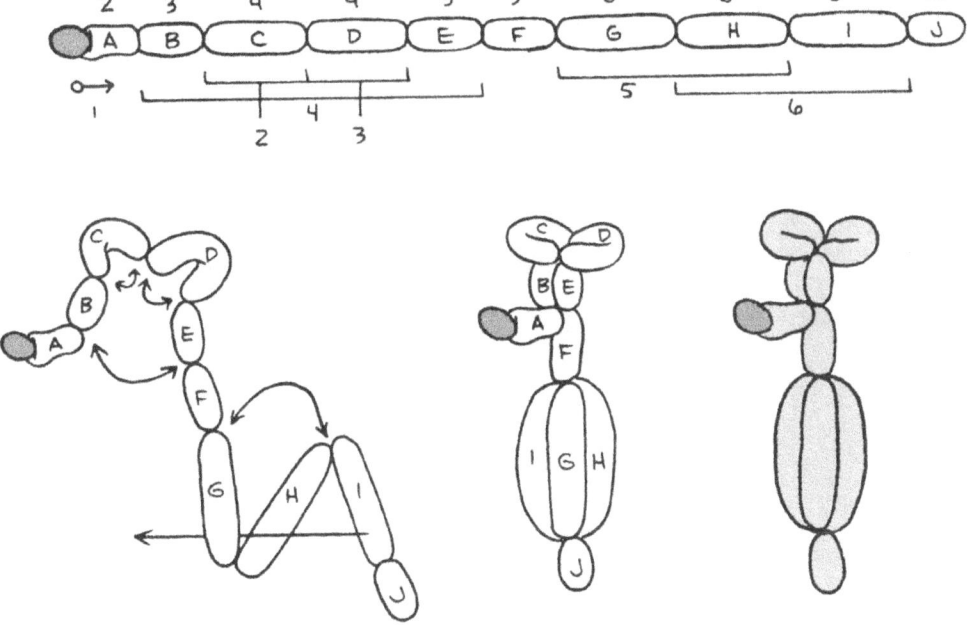

BALLOON 3

Inflate a white balloon so that it is about six inches long. Tie a knot. Attach to the head of balloon 2 as shown. Remove excess balloon by using a safety bubble. These are Rudolph's eyes!

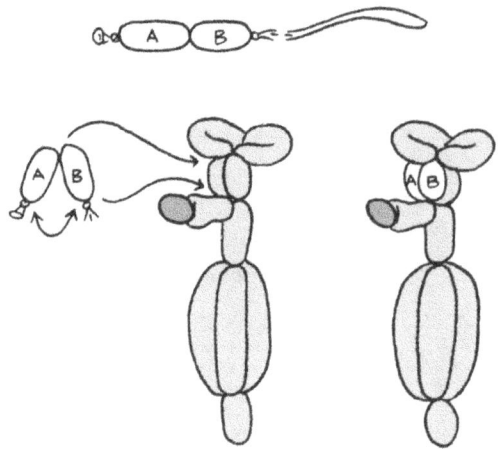

BALLOON 4

Inflate a black balloon, leaving about one to two inches of tail. Tie the knot. Complete as shown and attach to the head, forming Rudolph's antlers.

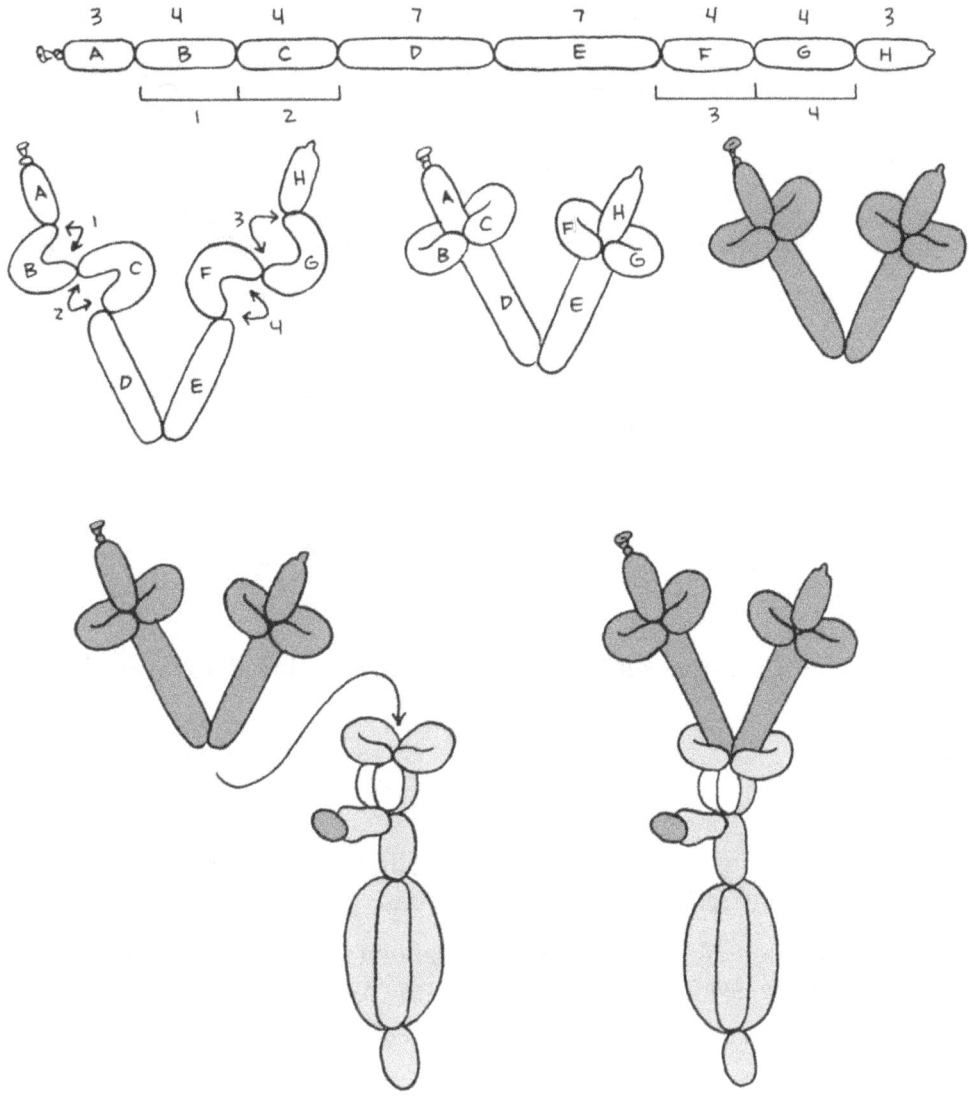

BALLOONS 5 AND 6

Make arms and legs out of the remaining two brown balloons. Attach the arms and legs to the body as shown.

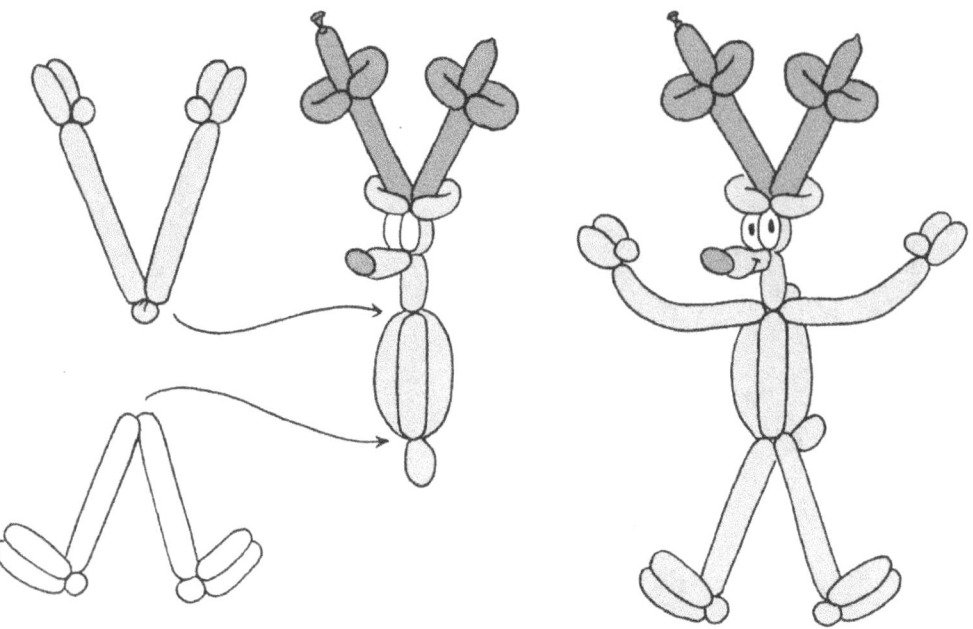

Add black pupils to the white eyes with a permanent marker and Rudolph is ready to lead Santa's sleigh!

MARTIAN

This last design is my favorite Martian, which takes a slightly different approach to constructing a cartoon figure. This design requires only three balloons.

Balloon 1 is not a 260. It is a 345, which is a wider balloon with a three-inch diameter. The added width eliminates the need to use a roll-through to create volume in the head and body of the Martian.

BALLOON 1

Inflate the 345, leaving about two to three inches of tail. Tie the knot.

BALLOONS 2 AND 3

These balloons are both 260s. Inflate them both, leaving about one inch of tail. Tie the knots. Make arms and legs out of these two balloons.

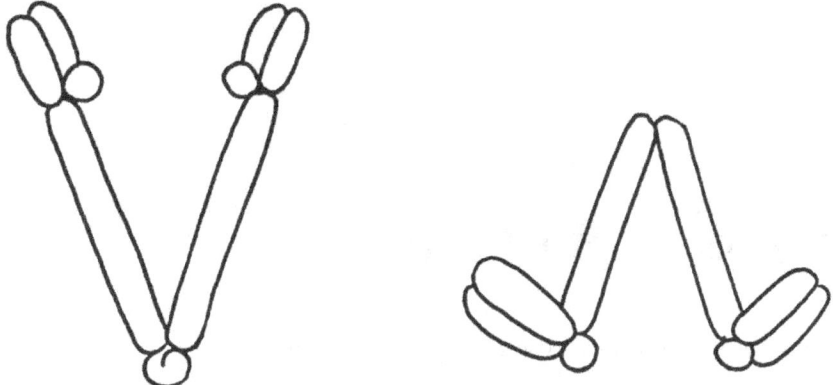

Attach the arms and legs as shown. Add a pom-pom to the head of the Martian to make an antenna. He's one spacey guy that is super quick to make!

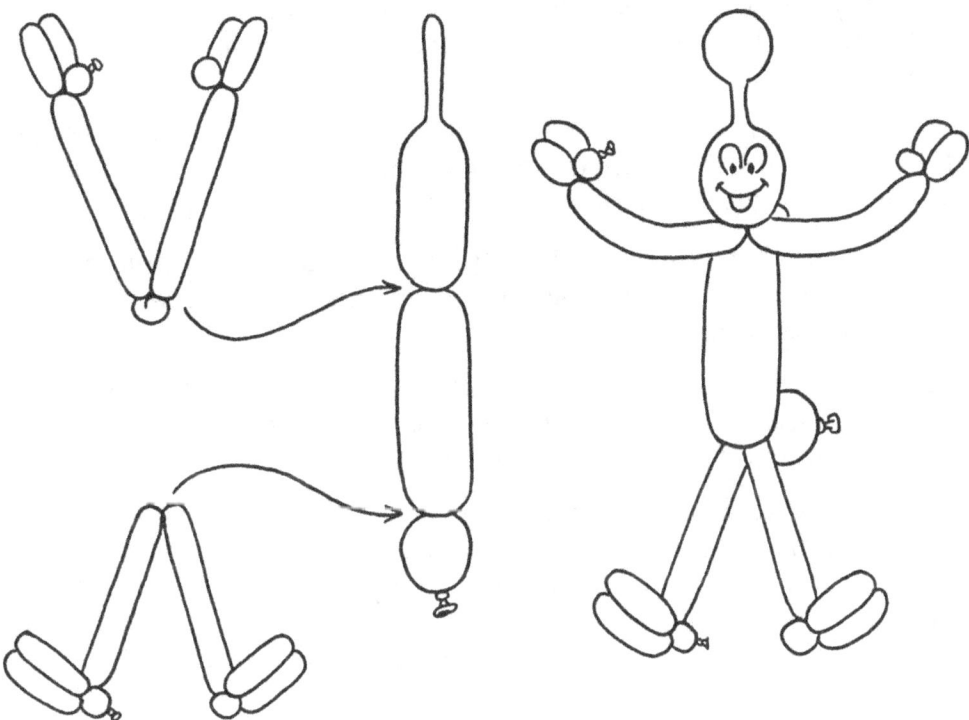

Chapter Fourteen

The Business of Balloons

Hopefully you have begun to realize the tons of fun you can have making balloon designs. You can spend hours playing with balloons, experimenting and designing your own creations. After you have spent some time practicing, you will get as much enjoyment out of impressing your friends with your balloons as you did twisting them for yourself.

The more balloons you make, the more other people will want them. Eventually you will discover that this new skill of yours is marketable and that people will want to pay you to entertain them with balloons!

Making money with balloons may not be for everyone, and indeed many people find enough reward with the enjoyment they get from balloons as a hobby. Those that are willing to venture into business with their balloon skills, however, can find it to be very fun and profitable.

Clowns, magicians, and other entertainers learn balloon skills to broaden their range of talents. It is not necessary to be an entertainer to make money with balloons, but it helps to be entertaining while you are making balloons for money.

There are four basic ways to make money with balloons. You can work for tips, be a vendor, be a decorator, or include them as part of your performance as an entertainer. All require skill, effort, and dedication for the balloon artist to be successful.

In this chapter we will examine these four different markets for the balloon artist. Each market has its own unique characteristics and requires a particular approach for the artist to be successful. They all also have overlapping qualities. It is possible for the balloon artist to capitalize on all of the markets and be successful in each. Most artists, however, find themselves comfortable with one or two of the markets and limit themselves to those.

WORKING FOR TIPS

Working for tips is possibly the easiest way to make money with balloons if you are starting from scratch. It requires very little money to start. You do not need to advertise, pay rent, have a phone, or hire employees. All you need are plenty of balloons, a pump, a neat presentation, something to collect the tips in, and, of course, some balloon skill.

There are two venues in which you can work for tips: on the street or in an establishment such as a restaurant or a nightclub. When you work the street, you rely solely on the tips for your income. When you work in an establishment, usually you will receive some type of fee for working, which is supplemented by the tips you make from the patrons. It is possible to have the bulk of your income come from the tips you receive.

The most important thing about working the street is location. You must find an area that has heavy foot traffic. Ideally, the people in the crowd should be families. Tourist locations are usually well suited for this, as are parks, shopping districts, and malls. Most cities have areas where many people go to relax and enjoy the sights. Learn your area and seek out the perfect location.

Be aware of local ordinances about street performers and vendors. If necessary, apply for a permit to operate in the area you find most desirable. Realize that once you set up, you may attract a large crowd, so be careful to pick a location where you will not obstruct traffic or nearby businesses.

Be conscious of other street performers and vendors. If there are others in the area, that may be a good sign that the area is profitable, but be courteous! Do not infringe on their business. Some areas may be able to support more than one balloon artist, but be careful to give each other space and the opportunity to succeed. Make an effort to become friendly with and be recognized by other vendors, street performers, security guards, and police officers. A good relationship with them all will always be a big advantage to you.

Once you have chosen your area, set up. You want to station yourself so that you are easily seen, and preferably in the shade. It is good to be able to have a wall at your back so that you know your group of customers will be in front of you where you will have better control of them.

Your tip container can be a hat, can, bucket, box, or anything else, but it should be prominently displayed with some signage requesting tips. Refer to paper money as much as possible with your signage. Deter coin tipping by posting pictures of bills or dollar signs.

Place a few bills inside of your tip container. You may want to have them fastened somehow so that wind cannot blow them out of the container, but you do want them clearly visible. You want the tippers to know that you expect something in return for your services and that you prefer it to be green and made of paper!

A few suppliers sell pins that encourage tipping with direct phrases like "I Work for Tip$" or "Tips Appreciated." Some pins have comical sayings that lightheartedly express your expectations. Prominently display these pins on your clothing. Your audience, hopefully, will get the message.

Always remember that when you are working for tips, you are vulnerable to cheap tippers and the occasional person who will stiff you by giving you nothing. You cannot let these few ruin your attitude. Most of the people you will encounter will appreciate your efforts and reward you accordingly with their tip. A positive attitude will result in positive rewards.

Now that you are ready to begin, you must attract a crowd. If they have not already begun to gather, start making balloons and give them away to the first handful of kids you see. Usually their parents are nearby and they will compensate you with a tip, but more importantly, the first balloons you make become your advertisement. They are walking billboards that the balloon artist is here. Your expense is a few balloons that cost pennies apiece.

Soon children and their parents will gather. I recommend that you have them form a line as soon as possible so that you have no doubts as to who is next. Parents will appreciate this because they do not want to see their child struggling to get your attention as you attend to a swarming crowd of kids.

Flashy big designs attract big crowds. Big hat designs are great at drawing crowds, because they fly high where everyone can see them. Big is best, but so is simple! If you are attracting big crowds, you want to move through them quickly so that they do not feel they've waited forever. Offer impressive designs that you can make quickly without the risk of a lot of breakage. Your happy crowd will be better tippers.

Sometimes it is best to work with a partner. You will have better control of the group and be able to produce balloons faster with two. Your partner can help the kids decide what they want by offering suggestions before the child gets to you. Some balloon artists use a "menu" with pictures of designs on a sign or a card that is either displayed or distributed among the group.

While you are producing balloon designs, keep a close eye on your tip container. You want to constantly maintain a minimum in the container so that it does not overflow and encourage theft. Remove accumulating money and put it in your pocket or fanny pack. Also, be aware of change that will wander into your container. Remove any change as quickly as possible so that you will not encourage more change by its presence in your container.

Many balloon artists that work the streets, or "busk," as it is called, create tip containers that absorb the tip. They do this by forcing the money into hidden compartments of the tip container, or by utilizing a slot for money to be dropped into. One of my favorite tip devices is shown on the right. It was made out of a rubber trash can that had wheels. The inverted lid doubled as my work station, containing my balloons and displaying some of my designs. At the end of the day, I could load my pump inside and just wheel it away!

Be aware of peak periods for your location. Whenever possible, arrive early to set up before the crowd arrives. Work until the crowd dwindles or you run out of balloons. If you become dissatisfied with the crowd for any reason (lousy tippers, too many wise guys, or you feel unsafe), end your line, pack up, and leave.

Do not count your money in public. Wait until you arrive home. If you chose your location well and you were personable to the people you made balloons for, you should be satisfied with the money you made. Good balloon artists can make several hundred dollars in one day, working for about six or seven hours in a busy area.

When you work for tips in the street, the crowd comes to you. In a restaurant, nightclub, or other establishment, you will usually go to the people, moving from table to table. You will want to use a very portable pump. A cup or a plate may be all you need for a tip container. You can wear pins that encourage the tip amount, and you can use menus to suggest designs.

When you are in an establishment, be aware of the other employees around you. Be careful not to interfere with their ability to get their job done. Stay out of their way and do not interrupt them when they are taking orders or conducting their business.

Restaurant and club work can be very rewarding. Often it can be a regular job, and you do not have to worry about the weather interfering as you do on a street corner. You can usually come by this type of arrangement by submitting proposals to the management of the establishment. Offer them colorful entertainment at a low cost and be sure to establish that you will be encouraging tips.

Balloon artists have to weigh their options and decide if it is more profitable to work for tips or to go into other areas of the business. In most areas, the tipping opportunities are seasonal and are always vulnerable to bad weather. Many balloon artists begin their careers by working for tips, then use the activity as something to fall back on after they establish themselves in other markets.

Whether you are working for tips indoors or out, hand your card to everyone you encounter. You will generate much more balloon work for yourself and most likely be propelled into the party business or one of the other balloon markets. Your card is your doorway to opportunity. Use it!

BALLOON VENDING

Vending as a balloon artist is very similar to busking. The major difference is that you are declaring a specific value for your work. Some artists have a price per design. Some charge per balloon used. Others have individual prices for each design, depending on the degree of difficulty and number of balloons used. Some type of chart with pictures of designs and prices is usually very helpful.

Balloon vending is popular at fairs, mall locations, flea markets, amusement parks, boardwalks, and other tourist locations. Most of the time, you will have to pay some type of rent or make some kind of equitable arrangement with the owners of the location. Some locations know the value of quality entertainment and find it to be a good trade.

Usually a commitment to vend requires long hours, but with reasonable prices the rewards should be great. It is not unreasonable to charge about a dollar per balloon used in the design. The average balloon costs less than a dime. Any retailer will tell you that is a great markup!

There are many vendors who sell helium balloons. These balloons require a minimal amount of effort and can be sold quickly. Vendors who sell twisted balloons, however, also sell entertainment and will generate large crowds that are there to be amused.

If you are an entertainer, use that to your advantage. Sell balloons in costume whenever possible and you will be your own star attraction. Most children will drag Mom and Dad over to see the clown or magician and then get a balloon as a souvenir.

Some vendors get the best of both worlds by making both helium balloons and balloon sculptures available. They can draw big crowds and sell balloons quickly, making the most money. Those that work like this usually have a partner taking money, conducting the crowd, and inflating balloons. They may have to split the money, but there will be more of it!

BALLOON DECORATING

Decorating with balloons has recently become incredibly popular. Most balloon decorating is done with round balloons and is a completely different style of balloon art, often requiring wire frames, string, adhesives, and helium. This is a highly specialized style of balloon art that may be for you.

Balloon distributors can give you information on learning this style, which is used to build room-sized designs that transform any environment into a fantasy zone. Much of this information is available free of charge because the distributors want to sell the large volumes of balloons that these designs require.

Many balloon artists use 260s for centerpieces on tables or for adding detail to the bigger designs. Some balloon decorators hire artists that specialize in 260 designs to do work for them because they may not be that familiar with the art of twisting balloons.

If you are interested in this type of work, contact balloon decorators in your area and make yourself available to them.

Some balloon artists like to create decorative designs like balloon flower arrangements, balloon baskets, or wreaths and make them available for delivery to loved ones that are celebrating an occasion or are sick and in the hospital. You can even be the costumed delivery person!

Advertisements in local papers, business cards, and word of mouth can get this type of business started quickly. Ask local businesses to display your cards or a small ad in trade for a free design. Many will be more than willing to promote your work.

USING BALLOONS AS AN ENTERTAINER

Most people love to have balloon animals at their children's party. If you are a clown or a magician, the kids will love the balloon gift that you give them. It serves as a lasting memory of the great fun they had with you.

Some balloon artists can entertain the entire party just by making balloons. There is so much you can do with balloons. Some balloon artists find the party business so exciting that they then learn magic and other clown skills, making them more versatile party entertainers.

Often balloon artists are hired at events to make balloons for all of the children. Some events are huge and it may take you hours to make balloons for everyone.

The entertainer will find that kids are not the only ones interested in balloons. There are many adult events where a strolling balloon artist is the perfect entertainment.

If you do a great job whenever you perform, everyone will want you at their parties. Keep a positive, happy attitude. Be sure to always hand out business cards when possible. Your entertainment business will grow and be very profitable for you.

BASICS

No matter where you plan to take your balloon business, there are a few basic elements that will help you succeed.

Know your market! It is very important, when you venture into a market, that you understand it. Are there enough people to support your business? How much can you charge? Are there potential customers interested in your services? Learn everything you can before you begin.

Know your competition. Learn exactly what services they provide, how much they charge, and the quality of their service and product. It helps to be friendly with your competition. Often they will refer work that they can't do to you, and hope that you will return the favor to them. Be fair: Price-cutting will hurt your business as much as it will hurt your competition's.

Know and respect the value of your service. A good balloon artist is a specialist with skills that are not common. Compare your prices with those of other performers with the same specialized skills to determine your fair market value. Once you have set your price, stand by it. Your customers will only respect and value your work if you do.

Advertise! Your customers will not know you are there if you do not tell them. Advertising does not have to cost a lot. Word of mouth is the best advertising, and it is free! Tell your friends, family, and neighbors about your new business. Make them a great balloon to take home and word will spread.

Business cards are cheap. Keep the information simple and clear, and don't forget to include your phone number. Give your card to everyone you meet, give them extras to give to friends, and your phone will ring.

When your business starts to grow, you may want to advertise in the phone directory or local papers, especially those that focus on children, parents, and families. These are great sources of additional work, but they require that you develop a budget to manage your expenses.

Another great source of promotion is the mail. Send promotional material to schools, churches, libraries, and local businesses. As your business builds, so will your mailing list. Send mailers to your customers on a regular basis to remind them of your services.

Be organized! Keeping your balloons and your presentation organized while you work will make the balloon twisting experience easier and more enjoyable for both you and your audience. There are many types of aprons, bags, rigs, and systems designed to keep your balloons separated by color, size, and shape while also helping to protect them from the elements. The type of setup you use may be determined by the style of balloon sculptures you like to make, the venues you prefer to work, and how mobile you would like to be. Many balloon artists use a few different types of systems to maintain versatility in their chosen markets.

Socialize with other balloon twisters! Get to know members of the global balloon artist community. There are groups that are easy to find on the internet; follow them and discover the vast and creative world they share.

THE LAST WORD

Twisting balloons is great exercise for your hands and the creative side of your brain. The skills that you will develop with the help of this book—and plenty of practice—are merely tools for you to become a better balloon artist. The many designs to be learned in this book are only starting blocks for your own creative journey.

Master these designs and you will become an accomplished balloon artist. Your skills will be impressive and you can be successful in any of the potential balloon markets. But you will always be a student, always learning new twists and ideas.

Look beyond these designs with your own creative eye. Borrow ideas and invent new ones. Develop your own designs and your own style. Express yourself with your unique balloon creations and you will become a true balloon artist.

It is through the learning relationship that balloon artists have with each other that our balloon designs, which may physically last only hours or days, can live forever. We pass them along, sharing our knowledge with each other, watching our designs grow and transform into new creations that will reach people the original artist may never even meet.

This has been the real beauty of balloon art for me, being part of the sharing heritage. Thank you for letting me share with you and for the opportunity to have my balloons, and the balloons of countless other balloon artists who shared with me, live on through you.

BALLOON SUPPLIERS

At this point, I am sure you are going to be so excited to twist balloons as soon as possible. You want to know where to get your balloons in large quantities and at better prices than your local party store.

The two most respected balloon manufacturers in the world today are Qualitex and Betallic. Each has a network of balloon distributors that sell their balloons and many balloon-related accessories made by other suppliers. You can order from them by phone or online, and they will deliver right to your door!

- Qualatex Balloon Distributors: https://us.qualatex.com/en-us/
- Betallic Balloon Distributors: http://www.betallic.com/DISTRIBUTORS/

Find distributors near you or distributors with the best prices or supplies for your needs.

For more information and inspiration, surf the internet for all things balloon-related, including groups, blogs, videos, clowns, and unique suppliers. Finally, look me up: Captain Visual: The World's One and Only Super Clown.

www.ingramcontent.com/pod-product-compliance
Lightning Source LLC
Chambersburg PA
CBHW081116080526
44587CB00021B/3619